"This informative, lively book is full of practical ideas. *She's Almost a Teenager* is creatively centered around important conversations every parent needs to have with their tween daughters to prepare them for what's ahead in adolescence. I highly recommend it!"

—**Cheri Fuller,** speaker and author
of *What a Girl Needs From Her Mom*

"Want daughters who behave the way you want when you're around? There's lots of advice that might help for a week or two. Want girls who learn to think wisely and confidently tackle life? Learn from the profound and practical question-asking guidance offered in this book."

—**Jim and Lynne Jackson,** co-founders
of Connected Families

"Do you have an 'almost teen'? It's time to drop the directives, and dialogue instead. The Larsons and Arps don't offer a big complicated plan. They provide something much better—conversation. If you want to get your daughter actively thinking rather than serendipitously slipping into the teens, you need this book."

—**Lori Wildenberg,** co-founder of 1 Corinthians Parenting
and co-author of *Raising Big Kids with Supernatural Love*

SHE'S *Almost* A TEENAGER

Other Resources From David & Claudia Arp

$10 Great Dates: Connecting Love, Marriage,
and Fun on a Budget (with Peter and Heather Larson)

10 Great Dates: Connecting Faith,
Love, & Marriage (with Peter and Heather Larson)

10 Great Dates to Energize Your Marriage
(book/DVD curriculum)

10 Great Dates Before You Say "I Do" (book/DVD curriculum)

10 Great Dates for Empty Nesters

52 Fantastic Dates for You and Your Mate

The Second Half of Marriage (book/DVD curriculum)

Answering the 8 Cries of the Spirited Child

Fighting for Your Empty Nest Marriage
(with Scott Stanley, Howard Markman, and Susan Blumberg)

The Connected Family

No Time for Sex

Suddenly They're 13—Or the Art of Hugging a Cactus

Other Resources From Peter & Heather Larson

$10 Great Dates: Connecting Love, Marriage,
and Fun on a Budget (with David and Claudia Arp)

10 Great Dates: Connecting Faith,
Love, & Marriage (with David and Claudia Arp)

The Couple Checkup (with David H. Olson and Amy Olson-Sigg)

10 Great Dates Before You Say "I Do" (DVD curriculum)

Great Dates Connect (DVD curriculum)

PREPARE to Last
(DVD curriculum with David H. Olson and Jeff & Debbie McElroy)

PREPARE/ENRICH: Customized Version
(inventory/assessment with David H. Olson)

Couple Checkup (inventory/assessment with David H. Olson)

SHE'S *Almost* A TEENAGER

TEENAGER

ESSENTIAL CONVERSATIONS TO HAVE NOW

Peter & Heather LARSON

David & Claudia ARP

BETHANY HOUSE PUBLISHERS

a division of Baker Publishing Group
Minneapolis, Minnesota

© 2015 by Peter Larson, Heather Larson, David Arp, and Claudia Arp

Published by Bethany House Publishers
11400 Hampshire Avenue South
Bloomington, Minnesota 55438
www.bethanyhouse.com

Bethany House Publishers is a division of
Baker Publishing Group, Grand Rapids, Michigan

Printed in the United States of America

Library of Congress Cataloging-in-Publication Data

Larson, Peter.
    She's almost a teenager : essential conversations to have now / Peter and Heather Larson, David and Claudia Arp.
        pages cm
    Includes bibliographical references.
    ISBN 978-0-7642-1136-2 (pbk. : alk. paper)
    1. Parenting—Religious aspects—Christianity. 2. Preteens—Conduct of life. 3. Girls—Conduct of life. 4. Christian life. I. Larson, Heather. II. Title
BV4529.L267 2015
248.8′45—dc23   2015015643

Cover design by Faceout Studio

15 16 17 18 19 20 21   7 6 5 4 3 2 1

This book is dedicated to our tween girls, Kate and Anna. Thanks for being such great sports and giving us so many stories to share with others. You are both a gift from God; we treasure who you are and are excited to see who you are becoming.

Thanks to all the parents and grandparents who have gone before us. You give us hope, encouragement, and direction.

Peter & Heather

Contents

INTRODUCTION

Welcome to the Tween Years:
Let the Conversations Begin!

Ten-year-old Elle announced to her mom, "If I had my driver's license, car, and apartment, I could live alone. I really wouldn't need a mother." She had always been a precocious kid, but this declaration got her mom's attention. Had puberty just begun? Was it time to batten down the hatches?

Too often our daughters' tween years are like a journey through a long, dark tunnel, and the only light to be seen is the oncoming train called adolescence! But don't panic. Help is here, both for Elle's mom and for you. In the following pages, we will help you prepare for and launch your daughter into adolescence. As you probably remember from your own tween and teen years, this can be quite a ride. It won't be perfect or smooth every day, but we hope to arm you with some helpful thoughts and direction for the journey ahead. First, let us introduce the team who will be your coaches on this trip into the world of adolescence.

Meet Heather and Peter Larson

We are right here with you on this journey, as we have tweens and teens in our own home. As parents of two tween daughters (Anna, age eleven, and Kate, age twelve) and a teenage son (AJ, age fourteen), we have treasured taking the time to write and talk through these essential conversations in our own family. Peter is a clinical psychologist and Heather is a life coach. Once upon a time, Peter was a youth worker and Heather taught fifth grade. We've had a lot of experience with children and have combined our professional and personal experiences to offer guidance and insight throughout this book. Gathering input from other families and working with Claudia and David Arp has been a blessing to us and will be an encouragement to you as well.

Meet Claudia and David Arp

First, a disclaimer. We have three adult sons and no daughters. However, for many years we have helped parents launch their sons and daughters into adolescence and navigate the sometimes turbulent teenage years. We founded PEP (Parent Encouragement Program) Groups for Parents of Teens and wrote the book *Suddenly They're 13—Or the Art of Hugging a Cactus.* So we can share the experiences of many parents who do have daughters. We have three granddaughters who, of course, are perfect. (Just kidding!)

For this journey, Peter and Heather will be leading the way, as they are in the middle of the adolescent years. Rest assured that they understand where you are, so you'll easily relate to them. Peter's training as a psychologist and Heather's as a former teacher and current life coach are invaluable in giving you helpful advice and support.

We will be the behind-the-scene supporters, and from time

to time will share some "Arp Adages"—tried and true principles—as well as practical tips from other parents who have successfully navigated this passage. Years ago Dr. James Dobson helped us prepare for this stage of life in his classic book *Preparing for Adolescence.* All four of us are standing on the shoulders of those who have gone before us. The Arps especially appreciate the wise counsel and advice from educators Bill and Kathy Clarke, who encouraged them to keep the lines of communication open and build the relationship with each child, and from Phyllis Stanley, who first shared the concept of preparing for the teen years through the vehicle of the Teenage Challenge (our Project Thirteen).

Our team would not be complete without you! You'll be amazed how much wisdom and insights you already possess. You may be part of a couple, a single mom or dad, or a grandparent or other guardian who is parenting an impressionable young woman. Whatever your situation, you might want to pull others into your support circle. You can use this book in a small group with friends who also have tween daughters, and challenge them to experience these important conversations with their daughters as well. As parents, you can share your successes (and redos when things don't go as planned) with each other.

You will discover that you are not alone in this process. You will also learn that each stage your daughter will go through is temporary, and each stage is leading to maturity! Thank goodness there is light at the end of the adolescent tunnel.

Why Conversations?

One truth that continues to rise to the top is the importance of the relationship you have with your daughter today. Although this book is for you as the parent to read, our hope is you will have new questions to start a dialogue with your daughter about the upcoming teen years. A conversation is an opportunity for you to be curious and really learn more about who your daughter is and who she is becoming. This isn't a typical parenting book with a "do this and expect this" kind of formula.

Instead, the following chapters include eight meaningful conversations, each crafted around a topic of interest to talk about with your daughter. These conversations are designed to help you both get ready for the years ahead. Reading the chapter will help you, the parent, prepare for a conversation to have with your daughter. We will look at the developmental process, biblical guidance, and plans for shifting more responsibility to your daughter as she matures. And for each conversation, we will provide questions and talking points for meaningful discussions together.

Conversation 1: The Big-Picture Talk

You'll talk about the shift that will be taking place and how over the next few years your daughter will go from childhood to being a teenager, and finally to adulthood. Together you'll talk through goals and the changing roles each of you will experience in the upcoming years.

Conversation 2: The Friends Talk

This conversation will focus on the natural shift in priority for tweens from family to friends. You'll have an opportunity to define together who she is becoming and talk about the importance of good friends.

Conversation 3: The Academics Talk

Together identify academic goals for your daughter during the teen years. Discover her strengths and challenges and plan together how to help her grow and reach her goals in school.

Conversation 4: The Body Talk

This conversation will help you navigate the upcoming wave of hormones sure to hit your home. You'll talk about body image, a balanced approach to food, and the responsibility of dressing modestly.

Conversation 5: The Faith Talk

Faith is the most important piece of who we are; it informs so many of our decisions. Your daughter will soon own her personal faith journey. Together, explore her plan for continuing to grow in her faith.

Conversation 6: The Boys Talk

Even though boys may not be a big topic yet, they soon will be! This conversation gives you both an opportunity to talk about the purpose of dating and describe the "dream guy." There are several thoughts to help your daughter stay pure in an over-sexualized culture.

Conversation 7: The Money Talk

One piece of independence is finances. This chapter will give you questions to help you discern your daughter's awareness of money and handling finances. You'll discuss expectations for future financial responsibilities and begin discovering your daughter's financial personality.

Conversation 8: The Tech Talk

In our culture, many parents are confused about the differences between rights and privileges. This chapter gives you a formula for how to handle technology (or any other privilege) using a series of questions to help you clarify the responsibilities and expectations associated with these privileges.

Project Thirteen and Birthday Boxes

This final chapter pulls it all together with two great ways to mark the transition from tween to teen to adulthood. Project Thirteen celebrates the arrival of the teen years with a creative opportunity for your teen to accomplish meaningful growth. The Birthday Box provides a clear road map for progressively releasing your daughter each year in several significant areas.

What's the Best Format? Weekly? Weekend Away?

What's the best approach for you to initiate these conversations with your daughter? This depends on you and your daughter's style and personality. Some of you may find that a structured weekly date works well. For others, a weekend away together is a great time to discuss the conversations introduced in the book. Perhaps you prefer a more casual dinner conversation by picking a question each week to introduce to the entire family with more personal conversations to follow.

What if your daughter is not cooperative? You're thinking, *She'll roll her eyes if I even suggest a special date.*

Know your daughter. Some children like the formality of a special date. Others think it's corny or may feel like a "big talk"

ARP *Adage*

Times with your tween daughter can be bonding times that help you focus on your relationship and convey the message that you are excited your daughter is growing up.

---

is coming. Some parents will choose to read the book and be ready to discuss the topics as they naturally surface in daily living. The topics are core to most tweens' experiences, so you won't have to wait long before they begin coming up. One parent said, "I knew if I wanted my daughter to cooperate, I'd have to make it really low-key. I never used the term *special date* or labeled the time as a tween conversation. Instead I would use opportunities to ask questions when we were alone in the car or other natural settings."

Get Started!

Your tween is quickly becoming a teenager. Fear not, help is here. Unlike other parenting books, there will not be a one-size-fits-all approach. Instead, you'll be challenged to think through questions and see how your answers fit you, your family, and your unique and wonderful daughter. Make it work for your family. If you feel the need to rephrase the questions so they fit your situation better, go for it. Write down your own thoughts and notes in the margins as you read through each chapter. Decide what topics, questions, and conversations you want to use. If something in this book doesn't fit your circumstances, feel free to skip over it. We want this to be helpful to you and your daughter and not feel like a forced or contrived experience. Our prayer is that these essential conversations will set you and your family up for success and joy during the teen years and beyond.

Conversation 1

• • •

THE BIG-PICTURE TALK

Begin With the End in Mind

"Where is my sweet little girl? Who has taken up residency in her body? I don't recognize this new attitude! She doesn't listen and questions everything. It's a full three years until she is a certified teenager. If she is difficult now, what will the teen years be like? Any help out there?"

Nervous parents are realizing the "golden years of childhood" are ending earlier and earlier. Their precious eleven-year-old is beginning to show symptoms of adolescence. They're scared. They feel unprepared. They're panicked and don't know how to prepare for the coming tsunami.

One parent gave an excellent challenge: "If you feel uncomfortable, embrace it!" In the following pages we want to help you embrace the coming years and develop your own balanced

19

approach to guiding your daughter safely into and through the teenage years and into adulthood. In each chapter we will frame questions to help you evaluate where you are in your relationship with your tween daughter, prepare for where you are going, and connect with her on a new level. These questions will be your guide for several essential conversations to have with your daughter now. Together, you can navigate successfully through the adolescent years and guide her toward maturity. Let's get started.

Conversation Suggestions

- Parents, start by reading the whole chapter before you start your conversation. This book is written for you; we don't expect your daughter to read it. Her only job will be to participate in the conversation with you.

- Consider each question, as well as the perspectives offered in the chapter, and be ready to discuss your thoughts on each question with your daughter. Feel free to take notes, underline, or adapt the question so it is worded in a way that feels most natural to you.

- Both the parent(s) and daughter are invited to answer each question, but we strongly recommend you let your daughter answer first. Give her the gift of being a good listener. Give her time to think, listen closely to her responses, ask follow-up questions, and respect her opinions. If you judge or criticize her answers, the conversation will quickly shut down. If you really listen and care about what she's saying, you're earning the right to be heard when it is your turn to answer. These are not questions that require quick or immediate decisions. For the most part, they are thought-provoking conversation starters.

"How Are You Feeling About These Upcoming Teen Years?"

I am nervous about my future teen years. I am nervous about my friends judging me if I make a mistake. If I wear the wrong clothes or if I say something wrong . . . will they still be my friends?

—Sydney, age 10

Excited! I can see our daughter has a strong sense of herself stemming from her fabulous relationship with her father. I never had that as a teenager and therefore looked to boys to provide that sense of security. I can already tell that my daughter has a better sense of who she is without needing attention from a boy to make her feel confident outside of her father and her brothers.

—Kristin, mom of a 10-year-old daughter and
her two big brothers, 15 and 12

I'm excited, but I hope I don't struggle with school and friendships.

—Brynn, age 12

Nervous! It is sneaking up way too fast and I don't know if I'm ready! I'm hoping that I haven't completely messed up as a mom and that they feel just as amazing about themselves as I feel about them.

—Jennifer, mom of four daughters ages 10, 8, 6, and 2

Concerned. I can't believe she wants to wear that! I know what boys are thinking!

—Craig, dad of two girls ages 12 and 10

Hopeful. Those years were incredibly hard for me. I had such a deep yearning for acceptance and tried lots of destructive things to gain it. My hope is in a chance to walk alongside my daughter as she navigates these rough waters and whisper in her ear how amazing she is and how much she is loved. I want to help her discover her strengths and find her voice. Most importantly, I can't wait to know the young woman she is becoming.

—Amy, mom of a 10-year-old daughter and 8-year-old son

Unsure. I'm not sure how to relate to my little girl, who looks more and more like a woman. Is she still *my* little girl?

—Jon, dad of a 14-year-old son and 12-year-old daughter

I am anxious and excited for the teen years for my girls. I remember a lot of hurt feelings and confusion around who I was and what I wanted to stand for during my teen years. I'm hoping my girls don't make the mistakes I made during those years. I want to be a good support for my girls, but I'm worried I could be too much of a helicopter parent and end up pushing my girls away.

—Rachel, mom of 8- and 12-year-old daughters and 15-year-old son

From the Parental Perspective

If you have wondered or worried about some of these same thoughts, you're not alone! Parents often feel the stress of the teenage years coming and are not sure how to respond. We love our kids and don't want them to face the same difficult experiences we encountered in our own tween to teen transitions.

One extreme is for parents to close their eyes and just hope for the best. The other extreme is to hold on so tightly in an effort to control their daughter that she has no other option but to jump ship!

One thing is for sure. There is a predictable tension between parents and their tween/teen daughters. Friends of ours compared their experience of raising four daughters with the metaphor of mountain climbing. Your daughter's job is to pull on the rope as she moves farther up the mountain, exploring and pushing herself. As parents, your job is to encourage her as you decide how quickly you can safely let out more rope. Climbers have a technique called "belaying," which exerts friction on the rope attached to the climber so they don't fall too far should they lose their grip. Just like belaying, there is healthy tension between parents and their daughters. When each is doing their job, it will result in some necessary friction. Rather than trying to figure out why there is tension, wise parents accept it and recognize it as something normal and needed.

"What is Your Goal?"

Parenting with your goals in mind will help you navigate the teen years. After all, you wouldn't typically head out in your car without having a destination in mind. Likewise, you want to know where you are heading as a parent. The road may have twists, turns, or detours you aren't expecting, but at least you have a sense of where you are going.

It is easy to agree that the number one goal of parenting is to raise independent and well-functioning adults. However, this goal seems to be taking longer and longer today, as more and more adult children are living with their parents after high school and college. According to a Pew Research finding, 36 percent of eighteen- to thirty-one-year-olds are still living with their parents.[1] There are several economic and cultural factors contributing to the rising age for launching children, but without clear goals around independence, it will be even easier for your daughter to move back into her familiar home, where the laundry is done, the refrigerator is stocked, and the cable TV is free.

To this day, I (Heather) remember the conversation my parents had with me about becoming an independent adult. They clearly communicated that after four years of college, degree or not, I would be on my own. I would be responsible for obtaining my own car and place to live. This meant I would need to have a job and a plan upon college graduation. Talk about motivation! I did not feel rejected or pushed out by my parents, but instead empowered, challenged, and motivated to be independent and successful.

While independence is an important goal, it cannot come at the cost of the relationship between parent and daughter. Be

As we examined our own parenting and that of our friends, we noticed three different styles of parenting. Actually, we can compare parenting styles with the way we nurture plants. Consider the following three profiles.

The Smotherer

The smotherer wants to stay in control and help the adolescent avoid mistakes.

Because of her fear, Erica shows a lack of trust and gives the impression that she is always trying to keep her daughter in the hothouse—holding her back as her daughter surges ahead toward independence. Just as plants that are kept in the hothouse too long become weak and root-bound, adolescents who are smothered may be unsure of themselves and unable to resist peer pressure. The teen who is held back may resent and reject her parents and their ideas.

The Pusher

An equally disastrous approach is to push your children out of the hothouse too soon before they are strong enough to survive on their own. Mike is a pusher. He expects his daughter, intentional about building and maintaining a strong relationship with your tween—it's a key factor in being able to successfully navigate the adolescent years. But it's extremely hard to develop that relationship during the teen years if you haven't worked on it previously. Build relationship with your children early. Do it now. Don't wait until later.

Peter has started by taking our twelve-year-old daughter, Kate, for a weekly date. They may choose to go for a bike ride or out for an ice cream. I (Heather) have found that most nights the kids will still let me tuck them into bed and pray together. This is often the time when our kids are willing to open up

---

Sarah, to become an adult overnight and gives freedom too quickly. His daughter doesn't have the maturity to consistently make wise choices and can easily become a peer-pressure victim. Where is the balance between being a smotherer and a pusher? Consider one other option.

The Releaser

Young seedlings must be acclimatized gradually to the new environment in which they will grow by allowing them short times in the sun and wind with temperature variations in the real world outside the greenhouse. They must have a "hardening-off" period. If the tender young plants aren't given this period to adjust, many will wither and die. However, if they are properly trained for survival in the new environment in which they are to grow, they will thrive.

Children also need a "hardening-off" period, which gives them limited freedom and increased responsibility under the watchful direction of their parents. Wise parents release them gradually. Your interaction with each other, which is greatly influenced by your parenting style and different personalities, will provide a foundation for helping your future teen enter the outside world.

ARP *Adage*

The challenge is to help her leave prepared to face life as an adult, and also with a positive relationship with you! So take the time now to set goals and come up with your plan of release.

about their day, ask questions for tomorrow, and let down their guard, allowing for increased connection. I'll never forget the first time I asked my daughter, "What would you like me to pray for you?" The answer revealed struggles I'm sure she would have not shared otherwise. Try asking this question and see what you learn about how you can pray for your daughter tonight!

In addition to having a great relationship with your adult daughter, what other goals are important to you? What are your goals for your daughter spiritually, academically, relationally, physically, or financially? We want to help you think through these areas in the upcoming chapters as you develop your own plan.

"What Should the Majors and Minors Be?"

Too often we tend to major on the minors. Having a clear sense of your parenting goals will help you identify what are the "majors" on which you will hold firm and what are the "minors" you can easily let go. Try asking your daughter today, "What are the things we as parents major on?" You may be surprised by an answer like this: "Always have a clean house, be on time, and brush my teeth and hair." Really?

If a goal is to focus on your daughter's character—respect, honesty, independence, strength in the face of peer pressure— how much time are you majoring on these things? It's easy for a teen to believe the majors are clothes, clean rooms, and less screen time and candy, when a parent spends the majority of conversation and energy on these topics. Through years of experience, the Arps have become experts on this topic of majors and minors.

Several years ago, we (the Arps) were the keynote speakers at a weeklong family conference. Most of our keynote addresses were to the parents; however, on this evening the teenagers were also part of our audience. But from the expressions on their faces, we could sense that they would rather have been anywhere else!

First, we thanked the teens for dragging their parents to this meeting despite their uncooperative attitudes. A few chuckles encouraged us to continue. Then we introduced the topic of majors and minors. "What are the things your parents major on?" we asked. Before we knew it, we had filled a chalkboard with everything from writing thank-you notes to eating breakfast.

Then we asked the parents what things their teenagers considered majors. It was obvious these parents and teenagers didn't live on the same planet! No wonder they seemed at cross-purposes.

Next we did something that at the time seemed risky. We asked individual families to dialogue together on what should be the majors and minors in their home and to do some negotiating.

ARP *Adage*

We need to decide on the majors because you simply cannot major in everything! Ask yourself this question: *Do the major issues coincide with what I am saying to my children every day, or am I majoring on the minors?*

But before deciding if an issue was a major or minor, we encouraged them to ask two questions:

1. Is it a moral issue?
2. What difference will it make in light of eternity? Or even ten years?

Amazingly, as we looked around the room, parents and teens were actually talking with each other! Later, several parents told us that this evening was the highlight of the whole week. Years later we continued to get good feedback. Some of the families got on the same page for the first time as to what their majors and minors should be. Such cooperation in families with adolescents usually doesn't happen spontaneously.

Asking yourself "What battles do I want to pick?" is another way to identify the majors and minors. Some topics to consider putting in the minor list may be clean rooms or hairstyle. You may want to save your ammunition for the more important battles to come. Wise friends of ours, Jim and Suzette Brawner, raised three amazing kids, so we were naturally excited to hear their thoughts on parenting as we were just starting our family. They told us about this idea of picking your battles. They identified three "majors" as they determined, choosing the three battles they were willing to fight. When their child made a request, they would ask themselves, "Is this dangerous, immoral, or illegal?" If not, they would often give their child the go-ahead. Filtering through these three criteria made it easy to know the answer if their daughter wanted to dye her hair blue or spend her money on some crazy new fashion. Since it wasn't dangerous, illegal, or immoral, the answer would be yes. Their daughter never did ask for blue hair, but their answer was ready. One youth pastor wisely said, if you can wash it out, cut it off, or grow it out, don't have a tizzy—it's not worth it!

Another helpful question the Arps encourage parents to ask is "What difference will this make in the light of eternity?" This powerful question brings great perspective. Your daughter does not need you nagging her over minor issues. Withstanding peer pressure, developing a positive attitude, and learning good decision-making skills are the more important issues of life.

Let us say it one more time: Major on the majors and minor on the minors. Some battles with adolescents are not worth waging war—plus you will lose the war. Psychologist Dr. James Dobson was asked why, when discussing adolescents, he focuses his comments on parents instead of on adolescents. He responded that when a teenager is about to go over the falls and he is intensely angry and is being influenced by a carload of crummy friends, it's the parent who can make the difference. In his newspaper column, Dr. Dobson cautions parents about being idealistic and perfectionists. It's easy to rock the boat. He writes, "Be very careful with him. Pick and choose what is worth fighting for, and settle for something less than perfection on issues that don't really matter." Dr. Dobson's good advice

---

ARP *Adage*

Your job as a parent is to work yourself out of a job and into a relationship that will last for a lifetime. By the time we had the answers to our kids' questions, the questions changed. It seemed we were always regrouping. The paradoxical statement, "We change in order to remain the same," certainly applies to parenthood and to parenting adolescents. We constantly change the way we relate to our children over the years. We didn't treat our eight-year-old the same as we did our toddler. But it all happened so gradually that we didn't realize we were changing in order to remain the same loving, caring parents.

applies equally to adolescent girls as to adolescent boys. He says, "Just get him through it!"[2]

"How Should Our Roles, as Parent and Child, Adjust as We Age? (What is My Role?)"

Each developmental stage requires different skills or roles as parents. Here are some ways to think about common stages and the roles parents can play in each season of development.

Newborn/Infant Constant Caregiver: When your daughter was born, she came into the world completely dependent on you as her parent to care for her every need. It is a parent's job to feed, bathe, and help her survive! These are the hands-on days of parenting that require twenty-four-hour vigilance. She depends on you to meet her every need. Care for her spiritually in these days as well by lifting her up in prayer. Many parents start praying for their child before they are even born or conceived. Do not underestimate the power of praying for your daughter. Prayer is key for you, your marriage, and your child to thrive!

Toddler/Elementary Age Teacher: As the baby girl grows and begins to toddle around, it is a parent's job to teach. Teaching how to do basic things such as feeding herself, walking, using the toilet, and brushing her teeth are just a few. Parents also begin teaching acceptable ways to talk, respond when given things, ask for things, and play with others. As your daughter

ARP *Adage*

Sometimes you need to simply listen to your children and save your advice for the family dog!

grows and heads off to school, she will have more experiences with other teachers, coaches, and instructors.

Through the elementary and tween years, your teaching role continues as parents teach how to handle simple chores, how to make choices in getting dressed, or decide what activities to try. Parents have an opportunity to teach family values and spiritual truths during these years. As your daughter is exposed to more and more instruction from others, you have the chance to talk about how to respond with grace when someone believes something you and your family do not hold to be true. Maybe your tween will start asking new kinds of questions about why you believe what you believe. Be honest and open to her questions. It will help you as you move into the next parenting role: parenting teenagers.

Tween/Teen Coach: A coach comes alongside and encourages, challenges, and guides someone. One powerful tool for a coach is asking open-ended questions, allowing a person to consider for him or herself what makes a good decision.

As a coach, try answering a question with a question: "Well, what do you think of that?" or "What do you think is the best thing to do in this situation?" It's easy to give instant answers, so as parents we have to check ourselves before we offer advice.

Coaching requires less talking, teaching, or "lecturing," as perceived by teens. Instead, there is more listening. A good coach will help uphold goals for her player, so when she is feeling discouraged or like "it's too hard," she has someone to remind her of who she is, where she is going, and all the help she has to get there. The teaching from previous years will help her remember these foundational truths.

Young Adult Consultant: As parents, your job is not over. The role of consultant is still important but requires less daily energy from you. A consultant is someone who your daughter may choose to call upon or not. Just like a consultant, she may choose to take your advice or leave it. She is now an adult and will be able to make her own decisions and choices.

Remember, prayer is important in every stage of parenting. Ephesians 1:16–18 says it well:

> I have not stopped praying for you, remembering you in my prayers. I keep asking that the God of our Lord Jesus Christ, the glorious Father, may give you the Spirit of wisdom and revelation, so that you may know him better. I pray also that the eyes of your heart may be enlightened in order that you may know the hope to which he has called you, the riches of his glorious inheritance in his holy people.

Adjusting our roles as parents can be subtle but necessary. Take for example one mom's experience of shifting her role. As a former teacher, Amy knew the importance of being firm yet loving with her kids. When her three children were in the toddler and elementary years, she knew how to direct and instruct her children. Her punishment was always firm and fair. There was no room for these kids to talk back or have a fit to change her mind. This parenting style was working great for these young kids who understood the word *no* and responded with respect and obedience. As her children grew, this approach continued to work well with her oldest daughter, who was easygoing and always a pleaser, but when the middle child, Hailey, turned thirteen, Amy noticed this firm teaching style wasn't working as well.

Here's the story. Hailey had been invited to go mountain biking with some friends. Her bike had a flat tire and her parents were out on a walk, so she decided it must be okay to borrow Mom's bike for the off-road excursion. When she got home, she found her mom was not pleased she had taken the bike without permission. To make matters worse, the tire rim had been bent on the outing and was going to require a repair and perhaps a new tire.

Without any hesitancy, Amy told Hailey her consequence would be to pay for the tire repair. Hailey wasn't too excited about this, but there was no talking back. It all seemed to be going as it had in the past: child misbehaves, parent gives natural consequence, child accepts consequence and hopefully learns valuable lesson and doesn't repeat the misbehavior. End of story.

Well, not quite. Hailey had been baby-sitting for a neighbor for an entire month in an effort to earn some extra money. She had been looking forward to taking the money and enjoying some outings with her friends at the mall. On payday, Amy came to collect the money from Hailey to pay for the bike repair. This is when the wheels came off!

Instead of obediently handing over the money to Amy, Hailey argued and pleaded. Finally, out of frustration, Hailey took off to her room and slammed the door, leaving Amy confused and frustrated. As a mom, Amy wanted her daughter to know she loved her, but she also needed Hailey to understand the importance of taking personal responsibility for making her mistakes right. She might be learning the personal responsibility, but she could see Hailey was not feeling loved at the moment. Amy realized she needed to try another approach.

After they both had some time to cool down, Amy invited Hailey to come sit by the fire pit in the backyard. She let her

ARP *Adage*

"A gentle answer turns away wrath, but a harsh word stirs up anger" (Proverbs 15:1). Before speaking, ask yourself, *Will what I'm about to say build up and encourage my child to grow as a person, or will it attack and tear down my child?*

know she would like to try a new method of communication where they each take turns sharing their thoughts and feelings as the listener reflects back what they hear and validates the speaker's feelings. First Hailey shared. Amy listened as she explained how hard it was to have worked so hard to earn this money for a month and how frustrating it was to just hand it all over for a bike tire. She felt completely deflated.

Then Hailey got a chance to listen as her mom explained how frustrated she was to come home from her walk and find not only her bike gone without her permission, but damaged upon return. She asked Hailey if she could explain how the tire got bent. Hailey had a chance to confess what had happened. She explained how she and her friends took a wrong turn and were stuck behind a fence. She thought she could just toss the bike over the fence and it would be okay, but it's probably when the tire got bent. It had been an accident.

Since much of Hailey's frustration came from having to hand over all of the money at once, she asked Amy if it was okay to give half the money to cover the tire and then come up with a payment plan to cover the rest of the cost. This seemed like a reasonable compromise to Amy.

But the best part of the story was still unfolding. After Amy took the time to really hear and understand Hailey's feelings and show her love and grace, while staying firm on her principle of responsibility, Hailey shyly asked to sit in her lap! This big thirteen-year-old wanted to be hugged and held. Hailey knew she was loved. She was no longer closed off in her room in anger and frustration. Amy saw changing her role from the teacher and instructor to the curious coach was the way to keep Hailey's spirit open and help her take ownership of her behavior.

······ CONVERSATION STARTERS ··············

You are ready now for your conversation with your daughter. Remember, you'll want to share your thoughts and hear your daughter's ideas about the following questions. These are questions your daughter may not have thought of before. It will be helpful for you to share your thoughts and excitement for these next years with her so she can start thinking about the transition from tween to teen as something positive too. A conversation is both of you talking. Ask questions. Share your answers to the questions and listen to her ideas. No one enjoys a lecture!

1. "How are you feeling about these upcoming teen years?" Be honest. You want your daughter to be able to share honestly how she is feeling. You may want to share the qualities and attributes you see in her that will help her navigate these upcoming years.

2. "What is your goal?" Share your hopes for your daughter and ask her to share her dreams too. She may not have thought much about these years. Encourage her to dream about them.

3. "What should the majors and minors be?" Ask your daughter what she thinks are the majors and minors in your family. Take this opportunity to share your goals and ways you could together let go of more of the minors and focus on the majors.

4. "How should our roles, as parent and child, adjust as we age?" This may be a tricky question for your daughter to answer. Start by sharing your role of shifting from being the teacher to the coach—wanting to start thinking things through together, empowering her to have some input rather than you always being the lone parental authority.

Conversation 2

•••

THE FRIENDS TALK

The Family to Friends Shift

Recently, I (Peter) spent a couple days out of town for some job-related travel. When I returned on a Friday afternoon, our twelve-year-old daughter was at a youth event with some of her friends. Kate texted us and asked if she could have a sleepover at her friend's house. We said yes and proceeded into our normal weekend routine. The next day, another friend called and invited her to go to a concert with her family at a mountain venue a couple hours from our home in Denver. It seemed like a neat opportunity, so again we granted permission. The friend's mom called later that day to say they were going to stay late for dinner in the mountains and asked if Kate could just sleep over at their house and come home in the morning. When she finally returned to our house, she was tired and took a nap. Upon waking, she was right back on her smartphone texting and socializing with friends. When we finally managed to peel her away from all this,

I felt like I was conversing with a long-lost friend! She, however, did not necessarily feel disconnected from the family. This pace of life is becoming her new normal. She is happy to be with the most important people in her life—her friends.

The picture is clear: Tween girls are increasingly more interested in friendships and less interested in their parents and family. Suddenly, friends' opinions become the absolute authority, even if they are coming from a thirteen-year-old. Friends will have growing influence on your daughter as she ages. This rising importance of friends in her life is natural and to be expected, even if it is confusing and frustrating at times. This influence is not necessarily bad or evil; it is simply a normal part of development as teens begin to crave more space and autonomy from their family.

Psychologist and director of the Laurel Schools Center of Research on Girls, Lisa Damour, used a metaphor to compare raising teenagers with swimming. The parent is the safe side of the pool, a source of stability and sure foundation. The teenager's job is to learn to swim in the deep end on her own. When the water gets too deep, however, the teen may cling to the parent, looking for assurance, comfort, and direction. These times can be full of surprising conversation and cuddling that may not have been experienced for some time. Gone are the one-word answers and cold shoulder. Parents are excited to feel reconnected with the once-distant teen.

However, when the teen feels ready to swim again, she pushes off hard, wanting to get far away from the edge of the pool where she may be perceived as a "baby" by the other swimmers. The push can be confusing and hurtful to the parent who has just experienced a close emotional moment. Understanding the push back into the pool isn't personal or against the parent as much as a pushing toward independence and adulthood can help during these often confusing transitional years.[1]

"What Does It Mean to Be a [fill in last name] Woman?"

In conversation one, "The Big-Picture Talk," you identified your goals during these tween to teen years. In this process, you may have noticed you have a list of family values you would like to pass on to your daughter. What attributes do you value? Words like *respect, honesty, perseverance, love,* and *kindness* may come to mind. Making this list is an important start. The next step is to find out what values your daughter already holds and what values still need to be taught.

Our family friends, Jeff and Gail, had a great tool to identify what family values "stuck" with their boys. When their youngest son turned fourteen and was headed off to high school, Jeff took all three sons on a camping trip. Jeff asked his boys, "What does it mean to be a Fray man?" The boys responded and agreed that a Fray man is a man of grace, lover of freedom, and contender for purity. These were the family values that stuck!

When I asked our daughters what it means to be a Larson woman, they responded with the values that have stuck so far. According to Anna, a Larson woman is smart, strong, beautiful, and kind. Kate wasn't sure if beautiful should be on the list, but wanted to include brave.

Knowing what our girls see as the attributes of a Larson woman helps us see what values have stuck and what values we still want them to "catch" before they are launched into adulthood. This process of naming the family values can also become an important part of their identity formation.

The Influence of Media and Friends

Girls are inundated with messages from a variety of sources about who they are and what they are expected to be. Advertisements on TV and movies are just the beginning. Now social media has found a way to advertise to young girls through YouTube videos by stars like Bethany Mota, who teach young girls how to dress, style their hair, and wear makeup. These "stars" have millions of young girls follow them through social media sites and meet them in malls across the country. Make no mistake, this is big business. According to a Piper Jaffray survey, middle-class teens are able to spend 30 percent of their money on clothes, compared to adults who typically spent less than 5 percent.[2]

Often the messages communicated through advertisements are if you look or dress a certain way, you will be happy and have the friends and attention you want. Other messages taught through our culture and media are more negative and destructive. Many images portray women as sex objects or that they're only valued for their bodies and looks. These messages are subtle but clear. Take the statement, "You throw like a girl." What image comes to mind? Unfortunately, "like a girl" has such a negative connotation that you probably picture an awkwardly bent arm, toes turned in, and an uncoordinated motion.

Peers make up another strong influence on your girl. As we've already pointed out, friends have some of the loudest voices in your daughter's ears during the tween years. The voices of her peers only seem to grow louder as they determine what's cool or acceptable in terms of clothes, music, relationships, slang, and behavior. Since this transition is so predictable, it is both strategic and important to talk about her choices in friends before the teen years.

One mom shared, "My daughter, Elle, has a friend who pulls her down. Her friend is a drama queen and from time to time won't talk to her. Recently she spread hurtful rumors about Elle. She also goes to our church, so her presence is even there." The girl strikes this mom as spoiled, often rude, and disrespectful.

"In trying to help Elle sort through her relationship with her friend, I asked her, 'Is this the way good friends treat other people?' and my daughter said, 'No, absolutely not!'"

Elle's mom continues, "While Elle's friends are more important than previously, she hasn't replaced me yet. Sometimes, to be honest, I think she has. But at other times I see she cares very much what I think. We feed off each other. I have to be careful to be the adult. Being aware of that can be a huge help."

Friends have the power to communicate all kinds of messages, either positive or negative. These messages are communicated with words as well as nonverbal cues. It can be the way the girls roll their eyes, where they choose to sit or not sit during lunch, or if they "like" your post in social media. There are so many ways to communicate, and teen girls are masters at finding feedback about their value or worth from other girls. Unfortunately, much of the feedback is negative or misinterpreted, and hence, a lot of the drama! Which messages will land?

POSITIVE MESSAGES	NEGATIVE MESSAGES
You are awesome and fun to be with.	You are so uncool and not wanted.
You are smart and creative.	You are stupid. You're a geek!
You are strong, capable, and athletic.	You should focus on being pretty or smart. I don't think the sporty thing is going to work for you.
You are kind and a good friend.	You can't be trusted because you are friends with . . .

Our daughters are inundated with messages of who they are and what they are worth during the teen years. Tragically, these are often lies to help marketers sell half truths whispered by insecure peers to make themselves feel better.

What Messages Does My Daughter Need From Me?

Parents have a responsibility to be the voice of truth, reminding their daughter who she is amongst the crazy din of media, friends, and school. What are the messages you want your daughter to know about herself? Make a list of them and share them with her. Some messages may include:

- You are fearfully and wonderfully made. (Psalm 139:14)
- You are a masterpiece and a new creation in Christ. (2 Corinthians 5:17)
- You are able to do all things. (Philippians 4:13)
- You are created for a purpose. (Ephesians 2:10)
- You have been set apart. (Hebrews 10:10–12)

Dr. Mary Pipher's book about adolescent girls, *Reviving Ophelia*, gives a current overview of the needs of adolescent girls: "While the world has changed a great deal in the last three decades, the developmental needs of teenage girls have changed very little. Girls need loving parents, decent values, useful information, friends, physical safety, freedom to move about independently, respect for their own uniqueness and encouragement to grow into productive adults."[3]

Here are some practical tips for relating to your adolescent daughter:

- *Give unconditional love.* Adolescent girls need parents who base their love and acceptance not on their daughter's performance, attitude, or mood, but on grace and unconditional love. One mother told us, "My daughter is having a difficult time growing up, so each morning I give her a clean slate. I erase all the hurts and angry words spoken yesterday, and give her the gift of a fresh start."

- *Remember that this phase is temporary!* Adolescence is time-limited. While some experts now say that adolescence may extend into the early twenties, it will come to an end. One day your daughter will be an adult. Let that fact encourage you and provide perspective when she is difficult in the adolescent years!

- *Concentrate on the relationship.* Our central message throughout this book is to keep building an open, honest relationship with your daughter. At times it will seem as if you are doing all of the work. Teenage girls can be especially caustic, haughty, and rude. Tolerate what you can and do all you can to preserve the relationship. At a critical point it could well be your daughter's lifeline!

- *Be brave enough to say no.* According to Dr. Pipher, research reveals the best family is the one in which the message children receive from parents is "we love you, but you must do as we say." She points out that adolescents do not deal well with ambiguity, so it's fine to establish limits.

- *Give a lot of affirmation.* Help your daughter make the most of her best features—whether physical or mental—and look daily for ways to give affirmation. Encourage her to keep achieving academically and, if athletic, to remain active in sports. Encourage her to adopt a healthy lifestyle, which includes a healthy diet. Whenever you can, give her an honest compliment. Whether you believe it or not, if she is like most adolescents, you are her hero.

- *Make a Positive List.* Use this verse as a guide and make your own Positive List. Here is our paraphrase: "Finally, parents, whatever is true about your child, whatever is honorable, whatever is just, whatever is pure, whatever is lovely, whatever is gracious, if there is any excellence, if there is anything worthy of praise in your child's life, think about those things" (adapted from Philippians 4:8).

"How Would You Want Others to Describe You?"

Stop now and answer this question for yourself as a parent. Did you list what you do, your job, or the roles you fill? Did you describe your personality or character qualities? We are each unique individuals who bring certain defining qualities with us. Other attributes are being refined in us through the power of the Holy Spirit, through time, and maturity. Let's look at a theory on personality and some thoughts about character and attitude.

Personality

You have probably seen your daughter's personality unfold since the day she was born. Maybe you were able to identify some of her personality even in the womb! When I (Heather) was pregnant with our second child, I remember sensing she was going to be a very independent girl. In fact, it was on Peter's birthday I knew I was close to labor, but almost as if she wanted to have her own day, she held on for twenty-four more hours. Sure enough, just past midnight our very independent daughter was born (two and a half weeks early). As a toddler, she didn't like to be held. She had too much to do and explore. To this day, she remains strong, courageous, and fiercely independent.

There are many theories around temperament and personality, and discovering your daughter's natural tendencies can be helpful during these tween years. Be careful, though: Many psychologists agree that personality is still being formed until around the age of thirty. Putting labels on your child can limit them or box them into being someone they are not.

One leading personality model known as the "Big Five" separates personality into five components, including openness to experience, conscientiousness, extroversion, agreeableness, and emotionality. These components are generally stable over time and appear to be attributable to a person's genetics rather than the effects of one's environment.[4]

Interestingly, these five personality factors appear to be consistent across cultures as well. Take a moment to think about where your daughter falls on these continuums. You might rate yourself as well and compare the ways you are similar or different. Consider asking your daughter to rate you too.

1. Openness to Experience:

   Conventional .... Progressive, Adventurous

2. Conscientiousness:

   Disorganized............................ Organized and Goal-Oriented

3. Extroversion:

   Introverted, Shy.. Extroverted, Social

4. Agreeableness:

   Competitive, Assertive.............................. Pleasing, Agreeable

5. Emotionality:

   Less Expressive, Calm .... Highly Emotional

Studying our kids' personalities encourages us to concentrate on their strengths and, at the same time, help them overcome their weaknesses. It also helps us as parents manage our own expectations.

Next, analyze yourself using the same grid. After all, you're part of this equation. So is your spouse. Where do you fall on the continuum? Take some time and reflect on how the personality mix in your home contributes to parenting/relational outcomes.

Merton and Irene Strommen (he is a noted research psychologist; she is a former public school teacher) said in their book *Five Cries of Parents*:

Poor parenting can result from a parent's unresolved personal problems. There are brilliant psychiatrists and psychologists who know a great deal about the human personality, but are inept as parents. Their insecurities and needs, obvious to others but not to themselves, profoundly influence their actions. Though insightful and effective when helping others, they lose their effectiveness when dealing with issues that touch their own lives. Having observed this phenomenon again and again, we find it crucial to encourage all parents to reflect on themselves as people and as a couple, as well as parents.[5]

Your personality will affect how you relate to your adolescent. Assess your own temperament and be as alert to your own tendencies as you are to your child's. Do what you can to understand your daughter and yourself, but remember to be flexible and open to changes up ahead.

Character and Attitude

Attitude is something you can choose each day. Attitude is defined as a settled way of thinking or feeling about someone or something. The thoughts or feelings are then typically reflected in a person's behavior, especially toward others.

Let's take mornings in our home (the Larsons): Our son has never been a morning person. He would rather sleep late, and even if he's up early, he does not want to eat or talk until after nine o'clock. Even though he isn't a morning person, getting up and going early is a necessity many mornings. These early mornings we've challenged him to choose his attitude and behave accordingly. He may not greet each family member with a cheerful smile, but he can still decide to be kind and gracious in his attitude toward others.

Character is also a choice. The moral decisions people make reflects their character. When thinking about character, attributes such as honesty, integrity, courage, respect, responsibility, diligence, and compassion come to mind.

If respect is important in your family, how do you treat others with respect? What do you need to do differently to model respect? Think through what respect looks like and feels like. Who is important to treat with respect: family, friends, teachers, pastors, strangers, cashiers, homeless people? Recently an adult friend asked us how to treat a brother who is choosing an affair over his family, which brings up the question: How do you treat someone with respect if they are not making choices or decisions you respect?

When I (Peter) was in practice as a therapist, I was working with a mother and her twelve-year-old son concerning some behavioral issues he was exhibiting at home and school. One of the recurring themes she kept bringing up was how she wanted him to respect her. As we unpacked some of their relationship patterns, it became clear that she often said and did things she later regretted, having lost her temper and becoming highly reactive to difficult situations. When complaining about wanting respect, she was very struck by the insight, "If I want to be respected, I need to behave in a more respectable way myself."

Think about the fruits of the spirit Paul describes in Galatians 5:22. These "fruits" are attributes God develops in people, and they are also attitudes or character qualities a person can display. A person can choose to be loving, joyful, peaceful, patient, kind, good, faithful, gentle, and self-controlled. Obviously, in

ARP *Adage*

The trouble with figuring out what our kids are like is that by the time we do, they've done another flip-flop. The only thing that you can count on during adolescence is change!

our own strength, we all fall short of this list, but with God's help these attitudes and character traits can develop in us. As parents, we have a responsibility to not only teach these attitudes and character traits, but to model them for our children.

One mom of an eleven-year-old girl shared, "My daughter is very perceptive. She knows immediately if I am stressed. She is continually watching what I'm doing rather than saying, and loves to point out my inconsistencies."

"Who Will You Hang Around With to Help You Be the Person You Want to Be? How Do You Choose a Good Friend?"

Often, girls are just discovering who they are during their teen years. Their personality may be developing, and they are making daily choices about their attitude and character, but they are still discovering their identity.

As adults, we can more readily identify who we are and what we like. Knowing these pieces helps us discern who will make a good friend. For instance, I (Heather) am a mom, a coach, and a friend who enjoys cooking, running, and being outdoors. I'm a positive person who enjoys encouraging others and being around other women who love God and aren't afraid to have fun.

However, when I was a teen, I wasn't sure who I was or what I liked to do, and had no well-defined criteria for identifying who would make a good friend. Recently, a tween girl put it this way: "If I don't know who I am, how can I find my brand?" Knowing more about who you are and who you are not helps tweens attract others who are like them and let go of friends who may be pursuing other priorities.

These friend groups may need to be flexible as teens grow and identify more clearly who they are becoming. Caroline had been a competitive swimmer who swam with an elite team and coach. Swimming practice or resting for the next swim meet consumed her days. She could see she was out of balance and wanted to find a team where she could still enjoy swimming competitively without quite so much intensity. By changing teams, she found more balance and a group of friends who also enjoyed having more balance. It was hard to release some of the friends who judged her for switching teams, but in the end she found her "brand."

Choosing good friends during the teen years is crucial. Friends can provide a great source of strength and accountability. Taylor moved to a new community at the end of her middle school years. The summer before high school, she made some wonderful Christian girlfriends. Taylor's parents got to know these girls and loved them too. They agreed to offer the girls a special trip at the end of their senior year of high school as long as they did not drink, smoke, or have sex before graduation. The girls loved this idea and got on board. Together they encouraged one another in the face of temptations at parties and in relationships. They had one another to talk to and ask for prayer. Without this goal, the support group, and the promise of the special trip, it was clear that one or all of the girls might have fallen into temptation.

Writer Josh Wiley has identified several passages in the Bible about choosing good friends:[6]

ARP *Adage*

Even though you can't choose your daughter's friends for her, you can help create an environment in your home where she feels safe and loved. The Arp Family Motto: On our team, we build each other up—there are plenty of people out there who will tear us down!

One who is righteous is a guide to his neighbor, but the way of the wicked leads them astray.

Proverbs 12:26

Whoever walks with the wise becomes wise, but the companion of fools will suffer harm.

Proverbs 13:20

A scoffer seeks wisdom in vain, but knowledge is easy for a man of understanding. Leave the presence of a fool, for there you do not meet words of knowledge.

Proverbs 14:6–7

Make no friendship with a man given to anger, nor go with a wrathful man, lest you learn his ways and entangle yourself in a snare.

Proverbs 22:24–25

Do not be deceived: "Bad company ruins good morals."

1 Corinthians 15:33

1. "What does it mean to be a [fill in last name] woman?"
   Let your daughter list the qualities she sees as important
   in your family. You may want to ask her about how media
   or friends might be sending her different messages. Tell
   her some of the messages you hope she will be hearing
   from you today and throughout the upcoming teen years.

2. "How would you want others to describe you?" Show
   her the personality categories and ask her to describe
   where she sees herself on each continuum. Let her describe where she sees you as her parent. Talk together
   about the strengths and challenges of each spectrum. How
   will your personalities relate with one another? Are you
   similar or different? Will these similarities or differences
   make things easier or more challenging? Discuss the differences between personality, character, and attitude. Ask
   her how she thinks others might describe her character
   and attitude.

3. "Who will you hang around with to help you be the person
   you want to be? How do you choose a good friend?" Talk
   together about what characteristics make a good friend.
   Remind your daughter that being a good friend will help
   her find good friends.

Conversation 3

• • •

THE ACADEMICS TALK

Academic Pressure/Stress

Mom confronting her daughter who got a less-than-stellar report card:
Daughter to mom: "Well, I'd never want to make all As"!
Mom: "Why not?"
Daughter: "It would be evidence of an unbalanced life!"

You may chuckle, but if your daughter gets As and Bs in school except for that C in French, you likely will spend most of your time talking about that C. Sure, she needs to work on French, but perhaps your daughter is just not great with foreign languages.

I (Peter) remember showing my report card to my father when I was a sophomore in high school. I had just completed a particularly successful semester and was bringing home mostly

As. I'll never forget my father's response as he looked at my grades and, after pausing, said, "Why don't you relax a little bit . . . get some Bs." Wow! This was not the response I had expected, but in retrospect it makes a lot of sense.

While eventually earning a master's degree in social work, my dad had been a C student throughout high school. He was more athletic than academic and spent more time with friends than books. His strategic thinking and relational aptitude, however, had served him well as an adult, and he eventually founded and ran a very successful business.

From his vantage point, my good grade in Algebra II was not as important as a manageable stress level. His life experience had taught him that high grades were not the lone predictor of success. I was fortunate because this type of parental climate took the pressure off. I was internally motivated to achieve, my father knew this, and there was no need for him to add unneeded expectations or pressure to my life.

Mary asked her seventh-grade daughter, Emily, what she liked most about school. Her quick response was, "My friends." Mary then asked her what she thought the goal of school was. Emily's response was, "To learn stuff." When asked about why you learn stuff, Emily said, "So you can be prepared for life." Mary thought this was a pretty solid answer, so she proceeded to ask if there was anything that gets in the way of "learning stuff," and she could only laugh as Emily's immediate answer was again, "My friends."

Interesting. Her favorite thing about school is also the very thing she perceives gets in the way of learning. Obviously there are some things Mary could address about disruptions or distractions coming from friends. But there may also be room for Emily to expand her ideas about the purpose of school and realize that her relationships with friends can play an important role in her future.

"What Is the Goal of School?"

How often do we stop and consider this question? What is the end goal when it comes to school and education? When we really pause and reflect on these questions, we may be surprised that we've bought in to a cultural lie. Consider the logical conclusions of the following hypothetical conversation between a parent and teen:

> "You need to work harder on that assignment."
>
> "Why?"
>
> "So you'll get a good grade."
>
> "Why?"
>
> "So you'll have a good GPA."
>
> "Why?"
>
> "So you'll be able to get into a good college."
>
> "Why?"
>
> "So you'll be able to land a good job."
>
> "Why?"
>
> "So you can make lots of money."
>
> "Why?"
>
> "So you can buy a house, own a car, and lead a comfortable life."
>
> Teen responds, "What if that's not what I want?"

Is comfort the main goal of education? Surely there is more to schooling than making enough money to be comfortable. Still, many just plod along in the educational system without ever asking *why* or *what is the end goal*. As we look deeper into the common goals of the Western educational system, however, some of the articulated objectives are more varied than academic achievement and carry much more meaning than just establishing a life of comfort.

Social and Emotional Development

An important artifact of school is the social interactions that kids experience. Learning how to handle conflict, deal with a demanding teacher, or navigate the politics of a clique are actually important life skills. Later in life, these skills will help your daughter solve problems with co-workers, deal with a tough boss, manage stress, and navigate her adult social life with increased confidence. Kids in school figure out how to interact with a range of personalities, ignore distractions, and foster close friendships. They learn to manage their anger, survive hurtful situations, and laugh with friends. They are put in situations where they must work in teams or deliver a project working alone. There are usually ups and downs in this social and emotional development process, but school is one of the few places where parents are typically removed from the situation, forcing kids to find their own way.

Homeschooling is a path that used to be equated with poor socialization, but twelve-year-old Bethany attends a homeschool group two days per week, which provides her with opportunities for social and emotional development with peers.

CareerBuilder.com conducted a survey of more than 2,600 hiring managers and found that 71 percent valued emotional intelligence over IQ. They believe those with higher emotional intelligence can handle high pressure, resolve conflict, lead by example, show empathy, and make more thoughtful decisions. In fact, 75 percent of managers said they are more likely to promote someone with higher emotional intelligence.[1]

Citizenship

It is easy to overlook the opportunities a student has for learning about leadership and service at school. Through activities like student council, clubs, sports teams, fundraisers, and special events, students are exposed to several important learning opportunities that are independent of academic achievement. They begin to identify and articulate the things they care about. Participating in these activities can give them firsthand experience with skills such as public communication, strategic planning, teamwork, organization, and leadership. These activities help them practice their people skills in real-world situations that translate well to community and occupational situations they will face as adults.

Vocational Preparation:
Competing in a Global Workforce

When we (the Larsons) moved to Colorado and enrolled our daughter in the sixth grade, we were surprised when they informed us she would need to have a certain laptop for school because all of her classes and homework were to be completed on the computer. We were not against this, but it was out of our usual paradigm. As parents, we want to be careful about fostering too much screen time. But in a world where both business and higher education are so reliant on computers, perhaps we should be grateful our schools are pushing computers and tablets into the daily academic flow. Nationwide, more schools are beginning to leverage technology and adapt coursework to better prepare students for relevant career paths. Some foster work-based learning programs that actually allow students to earn academic credits while working part-time through arranged apprenticeships or school-based enterprises. It is not an uncommon assignment for high school students to contact, interview, and shadow adults in the workforce to learn more about potential careers. These types of innovations speak to the role of school in preparing kids to enter the competitive global workforce.

Cognitive Growth

Perhaps the most obvious role of school is to foster learning. School education exposes kids to mountains of information, challenging them to understand, remember, and apply it. School should challenge your daughter to develop her study habits, memory, critical thinking, creativity, logic, and focus.

With these common goals in mind, you may want to help your daughter think about what her own personal goals for school could be. Does she have a sense of what she wants to do for a career? Does she know what she wants to major in at college? Is she solid academically but needs to work on making friends? Is she intelligent but has a hard time applying good study habits? Help her begin to think through how she can get the most out of school.

You may feel like your daughter is too young to be thinking about what she might want to do after high school graduation, but her choices in the next few years may impact her ability to succeed in her plans. Girls in the tween and teen years are most focused on the moment and often not thinking through how their choices today will impact their future. If her goal is to attend a college with the help of a scholarship, she may want to see what qualifications are required to receive such a scholarship. Often colleges are looking to see a well-rounded student instead of just academic achievement. Thinking through what other activities to participate in now will help her round out who she is growing into during these years.

"What Gets in the Way of These Goals?"

There are several variables that can interfere with your daughter's ability to achieve her goals for school.

Finding the Balance Between Too Narrow or Too Broad

If the only goals are good grades, then everything else could be considered an obstacle that competes with academic success. A single goal that focuses only on grades may be too narrow, neglecting other areas and creating an unbalanced life. As humans, we tend to focus on the areas we feel successful in and avoid things that are uncomfortable. While some girls will major in friends and avoid their studies, others can hide in their books and avoid social interactions as much as possible.

Often it is the parent, and not the child, who is overly focused on grades. Research suggests pressure is greater when parents focus mainly on the external rather than internal reasons for success.[2] In other words, if children hear the message that they must do well in order to get into the best college and have a prominent career, the stakes are pretty high. On the other hand, if students connect to the enjoyment, curiosity, and personal satisfaction that comes with learning and achieving one's potential, the messages are more balanced and the pressure more manageable.

Some families go too broad and have their daughters involved in everything: sports, music, theatre, dance, AP classes, and so on. While there are those amazing kids who seem to be able to do it all, focusing too broadly can create incredible stress. A certain driver of stress is to have more to do than you have time in which to accomplish it all. Sometimes it's kids who don't want to feel left out and sign up for everything they can. Other times, it is well-intentioned parents who don't want their daughters to miss out on any possible experience. Either way, going too broad can get in the way of doing fewer things with true excellence.

Finding a balance in life is key. Families need a balance between academics and other activities, but they also need to find balance in whose interests and energy drives the priorities. Claire had a gift for soccer. She was only ten, but she distinguished herself on the soccer field as unusually fast and coordinated. Her father was very excited about Claire's future in soccer and pushed her to try out for the twelve-year-olds' traveling team, even though she was two years younger than all of the other girls. When she didn't make the team, he was the one who was devastated. He pushed her to practice more in order to maximize her potential. Fast-forward three years and Claire quit soccer altogether, burned out by the pressure and unbalanced life. The priority expressed in her home had been soccer, not school. She was behind in her studies and had to work hard to catch up.

Achievement Versus Intelligence

An educational psychologist would tell you there is a distinct contrast between intelligence and achievement. Intelligence is the raw smarts a person possesses. When we talk about IQ, we are referring to one's *intelligence quotient* as indicated by a standardized test of some sort. Achievement, on the other hand, is what one accomplishes in terms of grades and daily successes. The moderating variables between these two concepts are tools like work ethic, organization, time-management, focus, and motivation. Some students may not be as naturally gifted with smarts, but they overachieve simply because of their raw determination and drive. Others are extremely intelligent, but underachieve because they lack the work ethic, motivation, or time-management skills needed to get things done with excellence. Lacking these skills can certainly inhibit your daughter's ability to achieve her goals, no matter how smart she is. While you can't really change someone's basic IQ, you can teach skills that foster high achievement. One can learn to be more organized and better manage their schedule. We can find ways to motivate an underachiever through various rewards and incentives.

"What Helps You Be Most Successful at School?"

Every student has a different academic personality when it comes to studying. This personality helps inform how your daughter will study and what parameters to put into place to help her be more successful. Ultimately, your end goal as a parent is to equip her to study and learn on her own, taking responsibility for her success in education. When your daughter asks for help on an algebra problem, it is an opportunity to teach her to use resources to help her solve the problem (using the book or online math sites), not just help her get the right answer on that problem. I often joke with the kids, "I won't be going off to college in your back pocket to help you, nor will you want me to!" It is important our girls are equipped to study, learn, and take responsibility for their education during the teen years.

ARP *Adage*

In an effort to build some of these foundational tools in our kids, we organized and hosted a study workshop led by an older student who had distinguished himself as a good student with a positive life balance. We are convinced our children responded better to an upperclassman's tips than they would have to their parents' prodding and direction.

When it comes to the best environment for school success, the answers will depend on your daughter's personality, goals, ability, and work ethic. You can think of your daughter's academic personality on a spectrum of sorts. And where she falls on this spectrum may dictate the best environment for her. Some girls are organized, goal-oriented, and super responsible when it comes to school. They are what you picture when you think of a straight-A student. If this is your daughter, perhaps her need is to avoid obsessing or putting too much pressure on herself. Her home environment may need to encourage a balance between academics and well-rounded interests and meaningful friendships.

On the other end of the continuum are kids who are disorganized, distracted, and not very responsible. They lose things, forget their homework, and struggle to focus on school. Sports, friends, or screens overshadow any sense of urgency to achieve in school. The optimal home environment for this type of girl will need to introduce more structure and motivation. She may need to be pushed and challenged to remove distractions.

	ORGANIZED DAUGHTER	DISORGANIZED DAUGHTER
BEHAVIOR STYLE	Goal-oriented, super responsible, overachiever, may be stressed or anxious	Scattered, distracted, loses things, forgetful, unfocused
NEEDS FROM HOME	Encourage more balance, less pressure, set aside time for friendships	More structure, increased motivation through consequences and rewards, help removing distractions

Our own two daughters represent various facets of this continuum. Anna (age eleven) can't relax until her homework is finished. When she comes home from school, she sits down and does her homework immediately with an internal drive and focus that needs no prodding from adults. Kate (age twelve) has always received good grades, but she can take thirty minutes of homework and make it last for hours, with several breaks and interactions that become time-consuming distractions. As parents, we often feel pulled to prod her into action or try to organize her efforts. At times, however, we may not be doing Kate any favors when we "over-function" for her.

A close family friend of ours has spoken words of wisdom on this topic of helping a less-organized child. He is a middle school science teacher who has been teaching for over a decade. In his experience, he has seen all sorts of students and all sorts of parents, but he is convinced that too many parents over-function for their middle school kids, working harder than the children themselves. While this approach may be well intentioned, it is only a short-term solution with long-term consequences.

One stressed daughter rushed into the kitchen and said, "Mom, I need help on my project!"

"What kind of project is it, honey?" her mother asked.

"It is a big social studies project. I'm supposed to create a map or model of an early colony, and I don't have any of the right supplies!" she exclaimed.

"When is it due?" her mother asked.

"Tomorrow!" cried the daughter.

Learning through natural consequences can be very powerful. Doing poorly on a project, or even failing a class, can be powerful natural consequences that can wake some kids up and provide the motivation they need to begin making changes. But when parents rescue their middle school child by doing half their homework, completing their projects, and organizing their backpack each night, they are actually creating dependency. They are working harder than their child! Comparatively speaking, the stakes are pretty low in middle school as things like class rank and GPA are not tracked until high school. If a child is to learn important experiential lessons through failing, it is better it happens in seventh or eighth grade as compared to sophomore or junior year of high school. As mentioned throughout this book, our job is to hand over responsibility and let our daughters own their journey. This is true in academics, just as it is in faith or finances.

"How Do You Feel About Our Family's Expectations About Grades?"

What Do Grades Mean?

When placing a value on grades, it is important to understand what grades actually mean. As a former teacher, I (Heather) believe grades are a three-way means of communication. The grade communicates what a student knows from their teacher to the parent. Some areas of content are mastered or understood, while other areas of content may need to be reviewed again. Grades also communicate the level of effort and responsibility of the student. Several missing assignments but great test scores communicate that the knowledge and understanding is there, but the effort is lacking. Grades are not meant to be an identity, as in, "She is an A student" or "She is only a C student." They are simply a form of communication about one small slice of a child's life and performance.

Looking at grades as a means of communication helps students, teachers, and parents know where to focus. A student who is lacking in effort and responsibility does not need tutoring in the subject, but she may benefit from some external accountability to help her finish her work. On the other hand, the girl who has all of her work turned in but is struggling to master the content may benefit from tutoring or online help.

If you view grades as a means of communication, try using it to open up dialogue with your daughter. When she brings home a test, start by asking her questions. Let's say, for example, she received a 75 percent or a C on the test. I always start with, "How did you feel about the test?" This question provides a ton of insight. If she responds she thought the test was super easy, the C might indicate a need for further questions about what type of grades she is aiming for. Perhaps she will share she is embarrassed by the C grade. She had thought the test was going to be covering different information and was surprised when she found she had studied the wrong material.

Another question to ask her after a test is, "What would you do differently to prepare for the test next time?" Again, depending on the answer, you may want to follow up with, "How do you plan to implement that change?" Helping her get specific on how to prepare for future tests, not just letting the answer go at "study more, duh!" will help her put together a specific plan (make notecards, try a pretest online, begin studying or working on the project sooner, study with fewer distractions, organize a study group, etc.).

Remember to focus on the positive grades too. Asking, "What are you most proud of on this test?" or asking, "What are you celebrating that you did well?" is a great way to encourage your daughter and let her see you recognize her efforts too. If she sees you acknowledge her positive efforts, it will increase her desire to keep it up!

Asking about academic expectations can be a loaded conversation. Where do your expectations come from? Are they realistic? Do they align with your daughter's interests and goals? Has she bought in? Does she share your expectations?

Consider Abbey, age twelve, who is going to a rigorous charter school, taking advanced classes, and working hard for her B average. She is smart but not necessarily gifted. Her work ethic and time management allow her to achieve this solid GPA despite the challenging curriculum. Her goal is to be the first in her family to graduate from a four-year college. Compare her to Maddie, age thirteen, who is in a struggling school district, taking easy classes, and coasting to an A average. This girl is intellectually gifted, but she's distracted by her friends and doesn't seem to try very hard in school. She has not yet thought about her goals for the future, but has a vague notion of going to law school someday.

At face value, Abbey is not getting the same high grades as Maddie. But it is obvious that Abbey is already working as hard as she can, and it is actually Maddie who needs to be pushed or challenged to step up her game. As parents, we must consider the academic context, a child's effort, her abilities, and her goals when setting appropriate expectations for her grades.

Our expectations will also be informed by what we experienced ourselves. Two great questions to ponder:

1. What did you like (and may want to repeat) about how your parents dealt with academic expectations?

2. What did you not like (and want to make sure you don't repeat) about the way your parents handled academic expectations?

Where to Focus?

My (Peter's) worst grade in college came in an acting class. I needed a fine arts credit, and my roommate convinced me to take Acting 101 with him. I've never minded public speaking, but I quickly found that getting into character and performing monologues was not my gift! To make things worse, I forgot about the one written exam in the course and showed up completely unprepared for the test. After bombing the exam, I had to rely on only my terrible acting skills to pull my grade up. In the end, I eked out a C. Aside from the ding in my GPA,

I bumped into some real limitations in my gifts and abilities. Despite spending many more years in school pursuing advanced degrees, I made sure that was the last acting course I ever took. Is it fair to expect good grades in every subject? There are times when a child is truly gifted in some areas but will struggle in others. Your daughter may be a natural artist and not a scientist. Or perhaps math comes easy, but she has a hard time with creative writing. These discrepancies in giftedness are sure to show up in her grades.

How should parents react to that one C amongst the As and Bs on her report card? Ironically, a common approach to education involves identifying weaknesses and then focusing extra time and energy on these areas, such as hiring tutors, taking extra study courses, and devoting all sorts of energy toward her deficits. There is a case to be made for a student to address deficits in foundational skills that will keep her stuck or hinder growth, but do we balance this by also fueling her talents and gifts? Today's common approach can feel like punishment if we don't also allow enough time for our girls to pursue their passions. Chances are she won't major in English if she has no aptitude for it. If we as parents can keep a good perspective on the full purpose of school, perhaps we can find more tolerance for a marginal grade once in a while.

1. "What do you think is the goal of school?" Asking your daughter to think through and define her goals for school at a younger age will help navigate future conversations around school.

2. "What gets in the way of these goals?" Think through what your daughter's strengths and weakness are around school. How will these impact her academic experience?

3. "What helps you be most successful at school?" Having your daughter name what she needs to be successful in school gives you an opportunity as parents to come alongside her to help her experience success instead of imposing rules for unclear purposes.

4. "How do you feel about our family's expectations around grades?" This invitation to dialogue gives you both an opportunity to share your thoughts around academics and hopes for the future.

Conversation 4

• • •

THE BODY TALK

Fashion and Physical Changes

At the mall the other day, I heard this conversation between two teen girls:

> "I don't know what was wrong with me today. It didn't matter what anybody did or said around me, I just wanted to bite their heads off!" one girl complained.
>
> "It's called puberty!" her friend replied as they both broke into peals of laughter.

"What's Happening With These Hormones?"

Your daughter may be too young to have any physical signs of puberty, but it is not too early to talk about hormones and how they affect the body and emotions. During the tween and teen

69

years, the pituitary gland in the back of the brain produces and releases hormones to signal to the body it's time to grow. Although both girls and boys produce estrogen and testosterone, there is more estrogen produced in girls and testosterone produced in boys. Increased estrogen can cause a higher level of emotional sensitivity while testosterone may increase anger and impulsivity. Unfortunately, the pituitary gland releases these hormones in unpredictable waves rather than a predictable steady stream, as Dr. David Walsh points out in his book *Why Do They Act That Way?*[1]

Perhaps you've already experienced something like this. You are talking with your daughter and everything seems fine. No big problems. Suddenly, she is near tears and extremely sensitive. On the outside, nothing has changed so it's confusing and difficult to understand what happened to cause this sudden change. You start asking if everything is okay. This seems to make things worse and she muddles behind her tears, "I'm fine! Nothing is wrong." The words don't match the behavior, and the behavior seems to have come from nowhere! This may be a moment when a surge of estrogen has been released into your daughter's body. You're confused. She's confused.

As a parent, it's important to step back and stop pushing your daughter to explain what is going on with her emotions. After all, she is as bewildered as you are and needs time and space to sort out her feelings. This is not the time to "solve the problem" or explain that her feelings are wrong. One wise dad of four girls shared his insight: "Adolescent girls need more hugs and less talking." We have found this to be very true.

After moving to a new state during our two daughters' tween years, one woke up feeling super sad. There appeared to be no apparent reason for the tears. When I asked her why she felt so sad, her response, "I don't know," seemed to bring another wave of tears. Even though it was a busy school morning and I

ARP *Adage*

The best time to prepare for the hormonal roller coaster is between the ages of eight and twelve, before the intensive changes of adolescence kick in. After that, just hold on!

needed to get everyone moving, I could see pushing her to talk about her feelings was not going to help. Instead of trying to fix her feelings, I sat and hugged her. We didn't talk. After a bit, she was able to stop crying and continue getting ready for school. We prayed together as she walked out the door, still not sure what all of the tears meant. When she got home from school, she seemed to be her cheerful self again. After a bit, I asked her what the tears might have been about earlier that morning. Her response: "I don't know. I think it was just hormones."

During these confusing years, having a basic understanding of what is taking place in the teen brain is useful for both daughters and parents. It gives everyone a language to describe what is being experienced. It's also helpful to have a plan for what to do when your daughter feels like biting everyone's head off or crying for no apparent reason. If she is open to a hug or just sitting together, you can try just being with her. If anger seems to be the emotion and she does not want anyone around, invite her to spend some time alone. She may want to go for a walk or listen to some music to help her calm down. It's key for parents to let her move through the emotional wave without taking it personally or telling her that her feelings are wrong. Remember, in the same way she can't control the surges of hormones in her body, she won't always be able to manage the waves of emotion she's experiencing!

Hormone surges may continue after the teen years. Perhaps as a mom, you struggle with PMS. Share with your daughter how you manage your own emotions. Do you take extra time for exercise or to be alone? One friend shared her personal monthly mantra: "Hormones make a good caboose but not a very good engine." She does her best not to make any major decisions when she knows her hormones are out of balance.

An excellent book dealing with hormones and the changing girl's body is *The Ultimate Girls' Body Book: Not-So-Silly Questions about Your Body* by Walt Larimore, MD, and Amaryllis Sanchez Wohlever, MD.

"How Do You Feel About Your Body?"

Emotional changes aren't the only changes to be expected. As you know, your daughter's body will be growing and changing rapidly too. Physical changes can start as early as age eight or as late as age fifteen. This can be difficult. At an age when girls want to be as much like their friends as possible, they may find themselves a head taller or shorter than the other girls in their class. Instead of looking like twins on twin day at school, they look a lot more like David and Goliath.

For the teen girl, this is not funny! Often these differences can feel like a real problem. "I'm a monster!" one beautiful teen announced while standing next to her shorter friends. Tall girls start to slouch. Flat-chested girls are tempted to add tissue to their padded bras. Girls will often believe "everyone else's body" is different or better. Then, just when it seems their body is finally okay, they wake up and find it still changing! Being confident in what your body looks like during these years is challenging!

Just trying to fit in physically with their friends is only part of the teenager's challenge. Models and movie stars have one-sized (tiny) bodies with perfect digitally enhanced complexions, straight teeth, and impeccable hair. When was the last time you saw a magazine with a plump and pimply teen or greasy-haired, gangly-legged girl featured on the cover? Um, never. Neither has your daughter, and she is looking!

One study found that 40 percent of nine- and ten-year-old girls have already tried to lose weight. The National Institute on Media and the Family reports that at age thirteen, 53 percent of American girls are unhappy with their bodies, a statistic that increases to 78 percent by the time they are seventeen. What pervasive lies our culture must be whispering to our daughters to convince 8 out of 10 seventeen-year-olds that their bodies just don't measure up to the standard of beauty.

Helping your daughter understand and accept her body starts with you. What are you modeling for her? How do you talk about your own body in front of her? Do you call yourself fat or complain about your long nose? Does she see you taking good care of your body? Are you constantly trying the latest

---

ARP *Adage*

Besides the predictable physical and emotional changes that occur in puberty, parents must also deal with the negative message today's culture sends to adolescent girls. She is to be pencil thin just when her body begins to round out. If she develops early, she is the object of sexual jokes and comments. Peer pressure adds to the cultural pressure from television, movies, magazines, advertisements, and school. No wonder she is sullen and secretive. In her excellent book *Reviving Ophelia*, Dr. Mary Pipher writes, "Early adolescence is a time of physical and psychological change, self-absorption, preoccupations with peer approval and identity formation. It's a time when girls focus inward on their own fascinating changes. . . . They blame their parents for their misery, yet they make a point of not telling their parents how they think and feel."[2]

---

fad diet? Do you binge eat when you are stressed? She is watching . . . what is she learning?

Reminding your daughter that her body is beautiful just the way it is during these years is essential. Remember, she is fearfully and wonderfully made! Every teen girl's body gets bigger and curvier during these years. Often her body will fill out before it springs up. Encourage your daughter to be confident in her body, with her curly hair or straight hair, her freckles or glasses. Be careful you are not modeling negative self-talk about your own appearance. You might even agree to ban the words *fat* or *ugly* from your home.

"How Do You Feel About Our Family's Eating Habits?"

What does food mean in your family? Is ice cream a reward for good grades or a win on the soccer field? Is going out for a treat a way to cheer or comfort someone when they are feeling down? Instead of seeing food as fuel, Americans often use food as a reward or consolation.

When our girls were younger, I (Peter) enjoyed taking them out for an occasional "special date" with Dad. We would often default to an excursion for a treat, such as ice cream or doughnuts. It occurred to me one day that I didn't want the girls to associate all of our special bonding time with sweets. I think some treats are fine, and I like ice cream as much as the next person, but we quickly found we could go to a craft shop, take a hike, go for a bike ride, or catch a movie on our special dates. This may seem like a silly distinction, but the subtle habit of always pairing quality time with sugary treats was headed in a direction that felt out of balance.

Our culture has become obsessed with food and weight. Think about the commercials on television. In one commercial break you'll view advertisements for fast food, then weight loss shakes, then the biggest developments in frozen breakfast waffles, and finally an advertisement for the latest exercise equipment. What are you supposed to do? Eat more? Diet? Exercise? Finding a healthy balance can be difficult, and we would suggest the pitfalls lie in the extremes.

Girls are not immune to the deluge of images as they watch movies, read magazines, search websites, and "follow" older teens on social media, looking for clues on how to dress, eat, and stay fit with the latest exercise trends. The messages can be overwhelming and confusing.

During these years it's important to communicate a healthy perspective about food and exercise to your daughter. Remember, she will most likely do what you do, not what you say. Your daughter may not trust your assurance that her body is beautiful and fine the way it is if you complain about being fat yourself or talk about other people's bodies this way.

While your daughter is still in your home, you have an opportunity to teach moderation. You may understand eating sugary treats or drinking soda is okay in moderation, but how do you help your daughter learn to apply moderation for herself without controlling the options and making the decisions for her? Next time your daughter asks for a sweet or treat, instead of just giving her a yes or no answer, try coaching her around the concept of moderation. Ask her to reflect on what she has eaten so far today. When she remembers she had two cookies after lunch and then a sucker on the bus ride home from school, you can talk about how much is enough sugar. After all, soon you will not be with her when she is choosing a snack out of the vending machine or the local convenience store with her friends and her own money.

Moderation also applies to portions. Teaching your daughter to eat enough fruits and vegetables to be healthy is as important as teaching her how much ice cream to serve herself for dessert. As she learns to manage her portions, teach her to consider a good balance between healthy foods and not-so-healthy fats and sweets. Again, someday she will face the dessert table at a buffet without you and will need to make her own choices. The teen years are full of constant changes, and many girls feel uncertain or out of control. For some, this is an age when they will use food and exercise to ease their fears and insecurities. They may overeat or binge eat to comfort themselves and then purge in order to relieve the guilt of the binge.

Other girls may try to control or restrict the foods they eat in order to have a sense of power in a season of life that can feel so out of control. Schoolwork is packed with pressure, "girl drama" is exhausting, and practice schedules are wearing her out! Keeping track of what and how much she eats may become one way to control at least *one* area in her life.

The challenge is to teach and model healthy choices and portions without obsessing about food or body image. Despite parents' best intentions, it is possible for the pendulum to swing too far in the other direction and girls to develop an eating disorder. As a parent of a teenage girl, you are not responsible if your daughter struggles with an eating disorder. It is not your fault. There are complicated cultural, social, emotional, and biological reasons some girls struggle with eating disorders.

One mom told us about her twelve-year-old daughter's friend who is anorexic. "She was at our home for dinner one evening and I noticed she only ate a few bites and said she wasn't hungry. My daughter has a healthy appetite, so this seemed abnormal. I mentioned it to my daughter and she told me that when she's at her friend's house, her friend usually takes a couple bites and says she's full." While her daughter was healthy, her daughter's friend was "skin and bones." Understandably they are very concerned.

Watch for these common warning signs and get help from a therapist and/or eating disorder treatment center if you're concerned:

- Constant adherence to increasingly strict diets, regardless of weight
- Habitual trips to the bathroom immediately after eating
- Secretly bingeing on large amounts of food
- Hoarding large amounts of food
- Increase in consumption of laxatives, diuretics, or diet pills
- Exercising compulsively, often several hours per day[3]

If you have a daughter who refuses to eat and is losing weight, act now to get help. An excellent book dealing with anorexia is *Help Your Teenager Beat an Eating Disorder* by James Lock and Daniel Le Grange.

"What's So Important About Clothes?"

A battle between parents and teens over clothes is not a new struggle. Here is a story my friend Angie just experienced with her daughter, Maggie, who brought home a top she bought with her own money while shopping with friends at the mall. To Angie, it looked like a regular sweatshirt. However, the next Sunday morning when Maggie came downstairs wearing the new sweatshirt for church, Angie was surprised to see how short the shirt actually was. When Maggie's arms were down, it was fine, but when she reached to get the milk out of the refrigerator, Angie could see her exposed stomach! This was something Angie was not prepared for, and she didn't know what to do. She asked her husband what he thought of the top. He only offered a distracted reply as he looked up from his laptop: "It looks fine to me." Angie was uncomfortable letting Maggie go to church and sit in a co-ed youth group wearing a top that might be distracting and show her tummy. And so the battle began. "You can't wear that shirt to church. I think it's too short." "It's fine. I just won't raise my hands too high. Besides, I bought it with my own money." "You're still my daughter and I can say what's acceptable for you to wear or not. That top is too short!" "Mom, you're so stuck in the old days! *Everyone else* is wearing tops like this. It's fine. (Insert eye roll.) This is the fashion. Besides, other girls are wearing things a lot worse than me!"

Having some clear rules before the situation arises may prevent some of the typical debates about what is *modest* versus what *everyone else* is wearing.

Gone are the days when you could clothe your baby girl in dresses and pink bows. As she gets older, your tween will have a stronger opinion and want a say in what she wears. Independence in dressing is important. You want your daughter to discern for herself what is appropriate to wear in various situations. Remember back to the discussion about what is a major and what is a minor issue. Use the following questions to think through now what is important for your daughter to know about making her own choices with clothes.

What Needs to Be Covered?

"Cover what needs to be covered and keep it covered" is Cynthia Heald's simple definition of modesty.[4] With today's fashion it seems less and less is being covered. Just look on the front of the magazines in the checkout aisle! Define with your daughter now what needs to be covered. Consider how long shorts and skirts need to be. Think about the sheer of lace fabrics. What kind of undergarment keeps her covered? What undergarments cannot be worn with a top over it? Are there certain body parts, such as the tummy, that should always be covered? Some clothes are so tight today that even though the body part is covered, there is nothing left to the imagination. How loose will clothes need to be? If wearing tight leggings, how long will the top need to be to cover what needs to be covered?

Is it Sexy or Lovely?

In discussing this topic, one mom shared a wise saying she had learned over the years: "Girls who dress sexy are looking for sex, while girls who dress lovely are looking for love." Of course, you want your daughter to look lovely! Most young tween and teen girls are not aware of the impact they are having on the boys around them. It is widely known that boys respond differently to visual stimuli than do girls. Studies have demonstrated gender differences in brain activity, neuronal pathways, and levels of testosterone in boys, all of which lead to strong visual stimulation and increased sex drive. Many argue this gender difference is unfair and wonder why girls need to go out of their way to *protect* the boys around them. Can't boys just use a little self-control? Of course this is a fair question. The facts about gender differences, sex drive, and visual stimulation remain, however, and it is important that our girls understand the unintentional effects their physical appearance has on the boys around them.

As a mom of a teen boy, I realize my son is responsible for his own purity. At the same time, the girls around him can make it a whole lot easier if they cover what needs to be covered and choose to dress lovely and modestly. As parents of daughters, we can help them understand that the clothes they choose to wear can show respect for themselves and respect for the boys and men around them. By covering what needs to be covered, they help a boy look at them as more than a physical object and see their real beauty. Short shorts, bare tummies, and low-cut tops only distract from her true identity.

What you wear impacts the way you feel about yourself and even the way you carry yourself! When you are wearing your bathrobe and slippers, you feel relaxed and may lounge in your favorite chair with a cup of coffee. When you are wearing a formal dress or suit with stiff shoes, you will sit up straighter and feel more proper. So when a girl chooses a sexy outfit, she may carry herself in a way that fits the dress. Likewise, in a lovely outfit that is comfortable and modest, she will feel more lovely, confident, and comfortable herself!

Who Is She Dressing For?

During the teen years, trendy clothes and the latest fashion are often ways to feel accepted or liked. It isn't enough to just have the latest shoes; they need to be the right brand too. The race to have the right clothes and latest fashion is a competition that doesn't end after junior high or high school. Girls will need to decide whom they are dressing for. Are they dressing to impress other girls so they will feel accepted? Are they dressing to catch the eye of a boy they like? Or are they dressing to express their personal style and please themselves?

The way we dress communicates many things. Think through how you make decisions about what you wear. You will choose one outfit for a funeral and quite another to go for lunch with a friend, one for working around the house and another for going on a date. What you choose to wear can reveal your mood and intentions and send powerful messages to those around you.

One tween mom shared her approach to teaching her daughter modesty: "I started emphasizing modesty when she was only two. Because of it, I'm not having very much resistance from her at twelve. When she dresses inappropriately I usually only have to say, 'That's not modest,' and she will change into something more appropriate. Often I will point out girls and ladies in magazines who are dressed modestly."

Physical changes are a big part of the teen years. Having conversations now while your daughter is young will help you navigate these upcoming transformations and decisions. Below is a list of conversation topics to discuss.

1. "What's happening with these hormones?" Remember, giving you both a vocabulary for the emotional swings caused by hormones will make riding the teen roller coaster easier for everyone.

2. "How do you feel about your body?" Your daughter is beautiful just the way God made her! This truth is easily lost in the teen years. Start reminding her today who she is in Christ.

3. "How do you feel about our family's eating habits?" Healthy concepts like *food is fuel* and *everything in moderation* are best taught now!

4. "What's so important about clothes?" Questions to consider together are: What needs to be covered? What is the difference between sexy and lovely? Who am I dressing for? Ask her how she feels when she is dressed up versus when she is wearing her pajamas. Clothes impact the way we feel about ourselves and communicate powerful messages to others. Start talking about modesty now.

Conversation 5

• • •

THE FAITH TALK

Internalizing Values

When we asked parents, "What do you want the most for your daughter?" some of the answers we received were:

- "That we would always have a healthy, open relationship with good communication."
- "That my daughter would own her own personal faith in God."
- "That my daughter would find a spouse with similar values—that family would always be important to her."
- "That my tween would know what she believes and would base her life on sound biblical principles."
- "That my child would be a well-adjusted adult and contribute to the betterment of this world."

- "That my teenager would be able to stand alone and make wise choices."

When considering the big issues of life, we didn't hear parents make comments like "I hope my daughter will always have a clean room and brush her teeth" or "I hope my daughter will never pierce her nose, tongue, and so on."

What do you think of when you look at the big picture? If you were to write a sentence or two on what you desire for your daughter, what would you write?

Cally grew up in a home as the youngest of four siblings. Her older sisters were eight and ten years her senior. This gap in age provided an interesting perspective from which to observe their spiritual journeys. For while she was still in a very concrete stage of faith development, she saw her older sisters question, resist, leave, and then return to their family's faith tradition. And while her sisters' beliefs were no longer identical to her parents', they had arrived at a solid spot. It was all quite bewildering to the younger Cally, and yet it somehow normalized the process of moving through her own journey of faith development.

The challenge in the area of faith and spirituality is for kids to transition from *borrowing* their parents' faith to *owning* their own journey. It is super important to educate and expose

---

ARP *Adage*

Consider this: If you trust God with your life, then trust God to help you with your daughter, who is on her own personal faith journey. We were able to keep going when we hit rough places because we knew God was totally committed to us and to our children in transition. We reminded each other what the psalmist wrote: "The Lord will perfect that which concerns me" (Psalm 138:8 NKJV).

children to the family's faith tradition, but at some point your daughter will make a decision for herself about what she believes. Keep in mind her journey is just beginning, and she is still a work in progress. With so many transitions happening in terms of brain development, cognitive abilities, social life, and hormones, don't expect her to have her whole theological worldview figured out at this age.

"Who Do You Believe God Is?"

This is a big question, and the way it is answered affects the very foundations and direction of our lives. Faith informs our identity, values, and decisions on multiple facets of life, including finances, education, relationships, leisure, and vocation.

James W. Fowler, a developmental psychologist, has written extensively about the stages of faith development in his book *Stages of Faith*. The model can be helpful in understanding some of what your child may be experiencing. While he outlines a seven-stage process from birth to older age, we'll look at the stages most relevant to tweens.[1]

Stage 1: According to Fowler's model, preschool-aged children (three to seven years old) are in Stage 1 of faith development and tend to learn about God through their experiences, images, stories, and people in their life. Sunday school classes for young children are designed around crafts, stories, and experiential Bible learning. In this stage, children reflect what they are taught and exposed to, mostly by their parents.

Stage 2: The next stage develops in school-age children from about seven to twelve years old. Kids in this stage will often have strong beliefs around justice and the reciprocity of the universe. They become more concrete about what they consider

---

ARP *Adage*

A wise friend reminded us, "If my kids buy in to 90 percent of my value system, I will feel I have done a good job of passing on my faith." Our children are not clones. They will go places we will not go and experience things we will not experience. Life goes forward, not backwards.

---

right and wrong, good and bad, and so on. This stage of faith development coincides with another famous developmental model created by Swiss psychologist Jean Piaget. One of his stages of cognitive development in children ages seven to eleven is called the *concrete operational stage*, which is marked by more logical thinking. The limitation, however, is that kids in this stage of cognitive development tend to be quite rigid in their thinking and struggle with more abstract concepts. Metaphors and symbolic language associated with religion are sometimes misunderstood. Somewhat like Santa Claus, God is likely perceived as a white-haired old man who is distant, keeping track of good and bad behavior, and not very involved in her life.

Stage 3: Your tween daughter may be starting to move into Stage 3 of her developmental faith journey, which typically begins around age twelve and will often last throughout adolescence. Thinking in this stage advances as kids begin to understand more abstract concepts. Girls in this stage have a deepening concern for others' points of view and a hunger for interpersonal relationships. The increasing importance of significant relationships is reflected in their faith as they now have the capacity for a more personal relationship with God, whom they may perceive as a cooperating friend. The opinions of peers will increase in importance as the opinions of parents are diminished.[2]

In summary, your daughter is on a faith journey that may evolve from a simplistic reflection of what she's seen and heard in your family, to a Santa-like old man who keeps score of right and wrong, and finally to a loving friend who is interested in her daily life. The model is a general overview, and not every girl will have the same experience or timing described above. Still, it is helpful to have some sense of the typical development of the faith journey so you can recognize some of the behavior and thinking you're seeing unfold in her life.

This question, "Who do you believe God is?" is indeed a big one. Remember, she is developmentally in somewhat of a bind. Part of her will feel the social pressures to conform, while her newly developing cognitive abilities can begin to question the status quo. If your daughter struggles to answer this big question, consider following up with some additional prompts like:

• What do you picture when you think of God?

• Where is God when you pray?

• What role does God play in your daily life?

• How does God make a difference in your world?

It is important to make room for doubts. Some church traditions imply that doubts or questions are a sign of a weak faith, and they should be squelched. Research, however, shows that as many as 70 percent of teens have questions about God and faith. Unfortunately, less than half of these students raise their questions with a friend, parent, or youth leader. When we accept and welcome questions as a normal part of faith development and provide young people with a safe environment to ask their questions or express their doubts, they actually feel more supported by God.[3]

"How Will You Continue to Pursue Your Faith?"

What are your hopes and desires for your daughter's personal faith? How will she own her spiritual disciplines such as prayer, tithing, and serving? What truths would you like to communicate to her? One friend, Gail, wrote each of her children a letter with her goals and desires for their spiritual growth. The kids read and re-read these letters of encouragement over and over through their teen years.

I (Heather) was super involved in church and youth group as a teen. I was *doing* everything right: attending youth group, volunteering, singing in the choir, and attending church every Sunday. You could find me at church more days of the week than not. I *knew* all of the right answers and believed them too. I just didn't know why.

My first year at college, when I took out my Bible, my roommate asked, "Why do you believe that, anyway?" Before this, I had not stopped to ask myself that question. My only response was an uncertain reply: "Because my parents told me to?" Needless to say, I was still *borrowing* my family's faith.

During the college years, I was actively (and at other times, not so actively) exploring what my faith meant to me. I needed to know for myself why I wanted to read the Bible and who God was in my life. I know this time of questioning and uncertainty was difficult for my parents to watch. Their patience and prayer without pressure allowed me to discover and eventually *own* the faith I have today.

Maybe you've heard the expression, "God doesn't have any grandchildren, just children." The shift from a parent's faith to her own is an important rite of passage. In a way, she *borrows* her parents' religion until she is old enough to think critically and form her own opinions. In time, she'll ask more questions, push back on the old answers, try on different ideas, and consider the grays in what used to be a very black and white world. Some girls do this very overtly and assertively, while others will quietly process all of this on an internal level. The questions for this conversation should help you begin to get a read on where your daughter is at on her journey.

One task for a parent will be to make this unfolding process okay and embrace the normal questioning taking place, without receiving it as a rejection or slap in the face. You may have already heard some of the questions: "Why does God let bad things happen to good people?" "If God already knows what is going to happen, what difference do my personal choices make?" "What difference will my prayers make to God?" "Where does it say that in the Bible?" and "Who wrote the Bible? Is it really the Word of God? How do we know it is accurate?"

Sometimes our urge in the face of our daughter's ambivalent questioning is to rush in and reassure her, attempting to provide solid answers and shore up the foundations we've tried to instill in the formation of her belief structures. Unfortunately, the more parents advance their experience of the truth, the more it can actually backfire as it simply gives her more to push against. Take heart, however—it is a normal and often necessary phase of her development. Instead, encourage your daughter to explore the answers to tough questions. Sticky Faith Curriculum published *Can I Ask That?* as a resource with a small group discussion for teens to explore just such topics.[4]

It's hard to relax when you feel responsible for things you can't control. It's hard to watch your tween struggle with faith issues. During these years it's good to remember the serenity prayer: "Grant me the serenity to accept the things I cannot change, the courage to change the things I can, and the wisdom to know the difference."

One dad used to stare at that motto, which was written on the wall of his church. He knew it was true, but he didn't want to admit that there were things in his life he could not control. Finally, he realized that so many things in his life were so out of control that he had to take the leap of faith and trust God for what he couldn't control.

While a parent may not be able to *control* their daughter's faith journey, they can certainly *influence* it. We (the Larsons) have found resources outside of our home that can speak into our daughters' lives. Youth groups and small groups at church allow adult volunteers and peers to unpack some of these difficult questions in a safe and loving environment. Parachurch organizations such as Young Life or Fellowship of Christian Athletes allow kids to explore faith in the context of their peers and friends from school. Even a week or two of summer camp, offered through a trusted organization, can provide a powerful and transformative experience for your daughter outside of her normal home environment. Maybe there is a book or an app that would help her on her journey. Pay attention and give her opportunities to explore her faith at a safe distance.

Don't underestimate the influence of family devotions. One friend shared how she had provided devotional material to her daughter that was age appropriate and attractive to tweens. Two such resources are *Girls of Grace Daily Devotional* and *Made to Crave—Satisfying Your Deepest Desires for God.*

"What Are Our Family's Expectations for Church Attendance and Activities?"

Our friends the Johnsons shared a typical Sunday morning in their house with their two daughters, Sara, age twelve and Grace, age fourteen. On a typical Sunday morning at seven, the house is still quiet. Their daughters are fast asleep because they were up late watching movies and hanging out with friends.

The Johnsons face a decision: church or no church today? They know if they wake the girls up and begin to rally the troops for church, it is probably going to turn into a battle. There will be complaining, stalling, and overall resistance. They've heard it before: "Church is boring!" "I don't like that youth group—none of my friends are there." "Seriously, that music is the worst!" It used to be easier. The Johnsons remember when their daughters gladly went to church. The girls woke up early, even before their parents, and were ready for the day. They were happy to go to Sunday school and hear the Bible stories and make crafts. Sometimes there were even doughnuts or bagels in the church lobby to provide the perfect reward for being at church. Now, however, they want to sleep in late. They are full of reasons to skip, and may even have other activities or sports that compete with Sunday mornings.

The parents have to cajole the girls into taking a shower and wearing nicer clothes. They may or may not have time to eat breakfast, and the whole family is stressed because they are all typically running late by the time they finally get out the door. Still, the Johnsons want to do their best because they desire to raise their girls up in the traditions and teachings dear to their hearts. It is often tempting to avoid the battle altogether and let everyone sleep in. But they remember the promises they made at their daughters' dedications, before the entire congregation, to raise her up *in the nurture and admonition of the Lord.*

For many, the scenario described above is familiar. But for some families, the flip side of the coin is true. Perhaps you are not connected to a church or place of worship, but now you have a child that wants to go. Maybe you had a negative church experience growing up and you've grown to generally mistrust religious institutions. But her school friends have invited her to attend an active church in your community and she likes it! This might feel unsettling and raise your concerns about the ideas and teachings to which she'll be introduced. How might this disrupt the normal flow of your family? At what age does she get to begin to make these decisions for herself? It may begin to sound redundant, but your tween daughter will increasingly want to control her own faith journey (and practices) as she grows up. For families who are trying to instill a faith tradition to a resistant tween, it can be helpful to give her some options that empower her with certain choices she can make for herself:

• Maybe she wants to sit with her friends in the balcony during the worship service.

• Perhaps she wants to attend the contemporary service rather than the traditional.

• Some tweens enjoy stepping up to volunteer with various aspects of the church (e.g., helping in the nursery or being part of the worship band) and are old enough to do it on their own.

Sometimes the choices will even stretch you further. We've seen kids who want to attend a different church from their parents because the traditional service does not feel as relevant to them as the upbeat service and vibrant youth group offered elsewhere. Some tweens are willing to attend a Sunday morning service with their parents but would rather plug in with a parachurch youth organization instead of their church's standard youth group. Perhaps your daughter will choose to explore some facet of her faith that is outside your comfort zone. It can be difficult to predict her path, so be ready to be stretched!

You'll need to decide what is required, recommended, or totally optional when it comes to church attendance. For those things you want to require as a parent, consider ways to communicate this message without being harsh or punitive. Once you've clarified the expectations, ask her how she feels about your standards in this area. Is she in agreement? Does she feel your expectations are reasonable? If she is struggling with what's been decided, try to empathize and keep the dialogue going.

Friday Pancakes

One of the best situations we (the Arps) experienced was when we were living in Vienna, Austria. Several wrestlers with Athletes in Action took an interest in our sons and in helping them reach out to their friends. Here's how it started. We were in a small congregation with no youth group, so we offered to begin one in our home. Every other Friday after school our teens invited their friends from school to come to our house for what became known as "Friday Pancakes." (Once the group was established, we substituted popcorn for pancakes. It wasn't so messy and was much simpler!)

The wrestlers took turns leading Friday Pancakes. Skits, table tennis, videos, and short talks on how your value system and faith can affect your life as a teenager were among the activities. But basically, the group was about having fun and providing a positive environment for our teenagers. The group grew, and we achieved one of our goals of providing a positive peer group for our teens as well as great role models. Now, years later, we still stay in touch with those inspiring wrestlers through Facebook.

Let us add, just in case you think relating to adolescents was easy for us, that when we first entered this stage of family life, we were very ill at ease with this age group. But this was a priority in our family so we worked hard to relate to our adolescents and to their friends. We did what we could to get our children into a positive peer group. We invested in them and their friends and had an open-home policy. We even spent that extra time and money to give rides to sports, scouts, and youth groups. Trust us, it is not always easy, but you can do it. Do your best to be available and flexible.

1. "Who do you believe God is?" Let your daughter explore this question with you. You will learn about her heart and be able to share yours too.

2. "How will you continue to pursue your faith?" Giving your daughter the opportunity to own her faith is a big step, but is necessary to make her faith her own. You can ask how you might help her continue to grow in her faith. Would she like a devotional book or other resource? Does she have a Bible that is age appropriate?

3. "What are our family's expectations around church attendance and activities?" Even though it may feel early to talk about this topic, you'll be glad you've brought it up so when the time comes it won't be such a battle.

Online Resources:
www.stickyfaith.org

Conversation 6

• • •

THE BOYS TALK

Boys, Boys, Boys

Boys may be the furthest thing from your tween daughter's mind today, but don't be tempted to skip this chapter. It is only a matter of time before your daughter becomes sucked into the world of crushes, dating, and prom!

"What Is the Purpose of Dating?"

Various books and resources will give you lots of suggestions on when and how to set up dating rules and boundaries. The idea is that you will release your daughter into the dating world slowly by starting with texting or calling boys, then letting her go on group dates, then double dates, and finally one-on-one dates. Many young people these days don't even talk about *dating*. Instead, they "hang out," "go out," or "hook up" in a

97

ARP *Adage*

Now is the time to decide how you will guide your child through the dating years, not later when you are faced with an emotionally charged situation and are unable to think clearly.

whole range of loosely defined and sometimes impulsive relational connections.

Whatever the dating policy becomes in your home, it is best to begin by identifying your beliefs about the purpose of dating. Beginning with the big-picture objective will help you decide when your daughter is ready to begin the adventure of connecting with boys and what boundaries are needed to honor the purpose of dating.

"What is the purpose of dating?" is a fun question to ask young girls and usually generates a variety of responses. It is helpful to consider what you both believe dating will accomplish.

Following are some of the lessons that I (Heather) hope our girls will learn through their dating experiences.

Be a Good Friend

Most young girls (up to age seven) don't have a problem being friends with boys. Being a good friend of a boy involves the same rules of being a good friend to a girl. Somewhere late in elementary school, girls can forget this truth.

Girls can use a variety of techniques to get the attention of a boy including flirting, teasing, ignoring, or even chasing. It is almost as if they wake up one day and look at boys through a new set of eyes, and don't quite know the best approach for interacting with boys anymore. There is a new set of rules and social structures emerging in her world. Reminding daughters how to be a good friend, ask questions, and be a good listener will help them practice their productive friendship skills during the upcoming dating years.

Let the Boys Pursue You

Growing up in a home with older brothers, our family dinners were often interrupted by love-struck girls calling my brothers over and over again. I saw how my brothers responded to this attention, and I learned I did not want to be a girl who chased the boys. I wanted to be pursued. Even after a first or second date, I would let the boy know he was going to need to initiate the call. This may have cost me a boyfriend or two, but I wanted to date boys who were willing to put some effort into the relationship.

Be Gracious

My hope is our daughters will learn how to respond graciously when a boy asks them on a date, regardless of how crazy she feels about him. She doesn't have to say yes to every boy who asks her out, but she should learn to be kind and respectful of the courage it took to ask. If he is a nice young man, I'd encourage her to

---

ARP *Adage*

Around sixth grade is when the phrase "going together" began to pop up in our home. I (Claudia) remember years ago when our sons started "going" with girls. Of course, they didn't go anywhere and rarely even talked to the girl they were "going with." Mostly they wrote notes, so I guess you could say it helped their writing skills. Today, tweens connect through texting and social media more than writing notes. They may have a new phrase for "going together," but the concept is the same: "I like you."

---

accept that invitation to the prom or homecoming dance, even if he wasn't her first choice. This doesn't mean she is committing to a lasting relationship, but she is honoring his effort and can be a good friend to a variety of boys along the way. She can also learn to set boundaries for herself in a kind but firm way.

Be Honest

Dating can go on far too long when one or both people are not honest about their feelings. I want my daughters to be honest with boys if their feelings have changed. Too often, people hold on to unhealthy relationships because they want to be sure to have a date for the upcoming New Year's Eve party or they are enjoying the attention they receive for dating a certain person. Being honest when feelings have changed is part of learning to be a good girlfriend.

"Who Is Your Dream Guy?"

Just as your daughter is growing and becoming who God has created her to be, so are the young men she is meeting. What are the attributes of the man you want your daughter to marry? Make a dream list and invite your daughter to make one too. Share your dream lists with one another and talk about why you chose the attributes on your list. Keep your list so when your daughter is excited about a new guy, you can refer back to it and see how he compares. This list can serve as an objective measuring stick in the future. Taking it a step further, have her brainstorm what kind of girl she needs to be to attract such a guy. What are the attributes she wants to have as a someday girlfriend?

My (Peter's) list for my daughters' future dates includes being respectful, hardworking, and trustworthy. If I'm going to trust a boy with my daughter, he had better be trustworthy! He needs to understand that she is priceless and deserves to be treated well. I've already been coaching our girls to never settle or put up with chronic poor treatment from a boy—no matter how cute or popular he is. But it is a two-way street, and the girls need to understand it is not all up to the boy's actions; she can set her own high standards of how to treat a boy and learn to honor them as well.

I also believe that the way a father treats his daughter begins to educate her on what to expect from boys. If a father is dismissive, rejecting, and preoccupied around his daughter, she will learn that she should not expect very good treatment from the men in her life. She may even begin to believe that she is not highly valued and deserving of love. A girl, however, wants to be noticed and pursued. If her father does not show genuine interest in who she is and who she is becoming, she will look for other boys to pursue and pay attention to her.

In summary, the challenge as a father is to "be" the dream guy and model the very attributes you would like to see her choose in a future mate. Treat her mother well, value your daughter deeply, be trustworthy, and treat her as a precious part of your life. Whether she knows it or not, she will begin to internalize these things as the norm for how her relationships with a man should work. When she bumps into a guy who doesn't treat her well, she'll quickly recognize it and know there are better options available to her.

"Should We (the Parents) Meet Your Date? If So, When?"

Some may feel it is an outdated tradition, but many families have the expectation that a boy who wants to date their daughter should come to her house and meet her parents. True, it may feel awkward and appear to be an intense requirement, but what does it communicate? To your daughter, it indicates that you care deeply about her and with whom she associates. It communicates that you have certain expectations for the boys she grants a deeper access to her life. To the boys, this requirement indicates that you are watching and monitoring what will happen in this relationship. It communicates that you care deeply for your girl and will go to great lengths to protect and stand up for her.

One friend, Scott, talked about raising his four daughters and walking them through this interesting journey with boys. The standard in their home was that you could have one or two dates with a boy before he had to meet the family, but if you were going to proceed in the relationship to a third date, the boy had to come and meet with Scott alone. It was not a huge conversation, mainly just Scott trying to get to know the young man and learn what he cared about in life. The unintended benefit was that his daughters would screen their own dates. This hurdle of having to bring him home to meet Dad caused the girls to stop and consider if her current date was worth the trouble. In many cases, the girls would end the relationship after the one or two dates simply because they couldn't picture a good scenario of the boy meeting their father. If, on the other hand, this was a high-quality guy she really cared about, it was worth facing the challenge of a solo meeting with dad.

Another dad, Sean, has his own approach to meeting his daughter's dates. If a young man wants a date, the first date is always dinner with the family. He believes a family dinner together gives him an opportunity to see how this young man interacts with his daughter and the other members of the family. A lot of one's character can be revealed during a meal together. Can he ask questions, listen to others, and hold a conversation? Does he make eye contact, have good manners, and articulate sound opinions? As mentioned above, the family dinner provides a hurdle for the daughter to consider. "Is this a guy I really want to invite over for dinner with my family?" If not, he probably isn't a great guy to date.

"What Is Needed to Stay Pure?"

Guard Your Heart

The Bible shows us how important our hearts are to God. In Proverbs 4:23 God commands us, "Above all else, guard your heart, for everything you do flows from it." The heart is the key to thoughts and feelings, which often lead to action.

Our culture carelessly uses the term *love* to mean desire, infatuations, attraction, or even fondness. Young girls easily shift from, "I like him, I love him, I hate him, I love him . . ." This roller coaster is no fun for anyone. I hope my girls will learn to guard their heart and carefully choose with whom and when to share it. Once the heart is shared, the body will often follow. If a girl believes she is "in love," she may use this excuse to justify a number of choices she knows are not best for her and her future.

Guard Your Eyes

It used to be we thought of pornography as something only men or boys struggled with. Unfortunately, with the Internet and ease of online pornography, young girls and women are exposed to and using pornography more than ever. According to a survey of more than 11,000 college-age women, more than half (52 percent) of young women today are exposed to sexually explicit material by the age of fourteen. According to a study published in *CyberPsychology and Behavior*, 62 percent of women have seen pornography by the age of eighteen. Exposures to porn during childhood are not just brief glimpses. Some teen girls are

---

ARP *Adage*

Adolescents can survive peer pressure much better when they know what they believe and have decided beforehand on their standards of action. However, even with this advance preparation, your daughter will at times be influenced by peers. But if you are communicating with her and are majoring on the majors, you can influence her today and build trust for the future.

---

viewing online pornography for a half hour or more at a time, and 1 in 7 have done this on multiple occasions.[1]

Talking about pornography with your daughter may be tricky and uncomfortable, but it is important to discuss so she knows what to do when or if she is exposed to it. Often pornography is introduced when another friend shares a site or image they have found. Pornographic images can also be found quite by accident. When looking for an image for a research paper, your daughter may type in an innocent web search and suddenly she is confronted with a variety of inappropriate images. Curiosity can take over and before she knows it she is down a trail she never knew existed. One mom of a four-year-old girl shared, "Accidental exposure to pornography and inappropriate images can begin at a really early age. My four-year-old loves to play a particular game on my iPad. Recently I realized it had commercials interjected into it. The game was age appropriate but the commercials definitely weren't! Periodically, I go through the settings and tighten them. You can't be too careful!"

If your daughter hasn't had a conversation with you about pornography, she may not know how to bring up the subject or even what to call her experience. Giving her a vocabulary and understanding of where it comes from is important in combating pornography in her life. God created us to be visually attracted to one another. Our bodies are designed to be beautiful to the opposite sex so we are drawn to one another. Unfortunately, this attraction has been used and abused to be something out of God's design. Pornography takes what God created for good and twists it to draw people into sin. Help her understand how destructive and sometimes addictive it can be so it doesn't become a negative force in her life.

Respect Yourself and Your Future Husband

Physical boundaries are important to establish and talk about before challenging situations begin to come up. A friend once compared physical boundaries to an upcoming cliff. Imagine sex is like a high cliff. There is a boundary fence twelve feet from the edge. Curiosity about the other side of the fence creeps in. There are friends on the other side talking about what's there. It's tempting to cross over the fence to get a closer look at the view and see what all the hype is about. It's easy to reason, *I won't get too close. . . . I'll be safe.* But sooner or later, you climb over the fence, and now the edge just doesn't seem as dangerous as it once did, so going right up to it doesn't feel like a big deal. Dancing along the cliff's edge, flirting with danger, a fall is imminent. What is the right distance for the fence to be protective?

One twelve-year-old girl received the following email from a supposed friend, who also happened to be her boyfriend's sister, pressuring her to "get with it."

Dear Emily,

If I had a boyfriend I would not let this happen! You are not getting anywhere (holding hands, kissing, etc.). Drop the shyness when you are around my brother. I say this because it seems that when you are around other boys, you're not at all shy! Could you tell me why? Well, okay, it's not all your fault. I have told him off too. If I were my brother, I would have dropped you long ago, but don't worry, he won't. Here are some tips for you—hold hands, kiss, hug, and talk to each other.

Stacy

P.S. Don't kill me!

As teens grow older, the pressure in boy-girl relationships only gets stronger. Dealing with a note like the one above is simple in comparison with being in a group where most of the other teens are already sexually active. A lot of teenagers start a sexual relationship only because of the peer pressure. Teenage moms who were asked why they started having sex almost all answer with reasons such as "I did not want to lose him" or "I was afraid to hurt him if I refused him." Add to the confusion the fact that some parents are neutral and others almost push their teenagers into sexual relationships, and it is easy to see how perplexing the relational environment of our teenagers has become. How can a parent help in the midst of this kind of peer pressure?

The sooner you start communicating, the better! Even at ten, eleven, or twelve, it's not too soon to be talking to your daughter. As awkward as it may be, talking with her about the pressure to become sexually active can open the communication lines and help daughters decide what their own standards will be. Parents can and need to talk to their daughters about sex. Consider the following statistics.

According to a survey commissioned by NBC News and *People* magazine of thirteen- to sixteen-year-olds, nearly 3 in 10 young teens are sexually active. Only 4 in 10 (41 percent) say they talk with their parents often about sex, while 62 percent say they talk to their friends about it. Older teens (fifteen and sixteen) talk about sex with their parents more than younger teens, as do girls more than boys. Parents were also polled but there was a discrepancy; twice as many parents say these conversations about sex happen with their teens (85 percent to 41 percent).

When asked where they get information about sex and sexual relationships, 70 percent say they have gotten some or a lot of information about sex from their parents, 53 percent say friends, 53 percent school, 51 percent TV and movies, and 34 percent from magazines.[2] We notice the Internet does not show up on this study from 2005. Certainly by now the web has become a major source of information for kids as well.

These findings are enlightening for parents who are trying to help their adolescents cope with a newly promiscuous world. If we want our teens to have accurate and value-based information, parents are the main source. We don't know any parents who say they want their teens to get their sex education from friends, movies, TV, or the Internet! These statistics encourage parents to talk to their kids about sex and be their main source for information.

God created each woman with a unique body, designed to be shared with one man in the holy relationship of marriage. Every time we share a part of our body with another, we can't take it back. After you hold someone's hand, you can't un-hold it. We give a bit of our body away when we let someone kiss or touch parts of it. This body isn't just yours. In Song of Solomon, it says that our bodies were meant to be shared with our beloved—not every cute guy along the way. This is difficult to understand when the hormones are surging and the message of culture says, "Just do it!" It is difficult, as television and movies seem to make fun of those who choose to remain pure.

Our culture has normalized the idea of living together before marriage. Many of you may have friends or family members who are choosing to live together. Your daughter may already understand what this means or will begin to in the near future. She may have friends who have a parent who is living with someone other than his or her spouse. It is not uncommon to see someone in your own family who is in a cohabiting relationship. Despite this trend of living together becoming the new norm, social scientists have consistently found that couples who cohabitate before marriage do not fare as well.[3] Dr. Scott Stanley and his colleagues talk about the difference between "sliding and deciding" when it comes to marriage. Unfortunately, couples who live together without a marriage commitment tend to intertwine their lives. They rent an apartment, buy furniture, get a dog, intermingle their finances, and some even have a child. Pretty soon, they figure, "We might was well get married," as they slide into the biggest decision of their adult life.

On the other hand, deciding to get married before cohabitating sends a very different message indicating "I choose you." The commitment levels, satisfaction, and long-term success of these marriages is significantly better. Having an open line of communication about your expectations regarding living together before marriage is important to establish before the question becomes an option for your daughter.

Be Smart

Recent news stories have been discussing the prevalence of rape and sexual assault in high schools and on college campuses.[4] One predominant theme in these stories is the correlation between drinking and date rape. When young girls get intoxicated at a party, with a group, or out with a boy, they are setting themselves up for serious trouble. One study found that a college girl was nineteen times more likely to be sexually assaulted if she had four or more drinks. If your daughter is serious about purity, you'll need to have a serious conversation about how sexual behavior is connected to drug and alcohol use in the party scene.[5]

Create Accountability

Remember when you were a teenager and out on a date? The emotions and nerves were on edge! When your daughter has a clear sense of what her boundaries are before she gets in a situation, she is better equipped to stick to her guns when the situation presents itself. Unfortunately, in some cases the pressure may feel too much, and it helps to know you have some external accountability in place.

We shared in "The Friends Talk" chapter about a family who helped their daughter set up accountability with friends: They all agreed to abstain from drinking, smoking, and sexual activity throughout high school. As a reward for their abstinence, they would take a trip together to celebrate their purity after high school.

Other programs, such as Passport2Purity by Dennis and Barbara Rainey, are a great way for parents to talk about purity and create accountability.[6] Some girls may even choose to wear a purity ring once they have made a commitment to remain pure.

Years ago, sex education went like this: Mom had "the talk" with daughters and Dad had "the talk" with sons. But that's ancient history. Serious talks make kids feel uncomfortable or like they are being preached at. They just don't work!

It is much better for "the talk" to turn into many casual conversations. Talking in the kitchen while preparing dinner is more effective, and you'll find your daughter is more open and less embarrassed. When a neighbor's fifteen-year-old became pregnant, one mom had the natural opportunity to talk to her daughter about the risks of having sex. Mom pointed out that instead of having a typical carefree university experience, her friend will probably end up living with her parents or marrying a guy she doesn't even really know.

Help your daughter come up with a ready response if she is pressured into having sex. That classic line, "If you love me, you'll have sex with me," can be countered with, "I'm not ready for sex, and if you really care about me, you'll respect my decision."

As uncomfortable as it might be to talk about sex with your tween, let us encourage you to keep talking. Otherwise, their information comes from uninformed friends armed with misguided values, or from movies, television, and magazines, which are totally unrealistic.

If you hear, "I know all of this already," and your kid tries to blow you off, just say, "I know you've heard this before, but I want to be sure you understand my views, and I want to know your views. I really love you and I want to be confident that we're on the same page." When all is said and done, remember you are still your teenager's major role model!

Now it is time for your conversation with your daughter. Talking about boys and purity may be uncomfortable for both of you. Try finding a comfortable setting where you might walk and talk. Even going for a drive can be a nice way to ease into the conversation and make it more comfortable. Some families choose to have a special weekend away together to talk about sex and purity.

You may feel like your daughter is too young to talk about some of the questions. Use your discretion, but be sure not to put it off too long. Often girls are thinking about boys or hear other girls talking about things long before parents realize it.

1. "What is the purpose of dating?" Talk together about why she believes dating is or is not important. Ask her what she thinks will be an appropriate age to start dating. Share your thoughts with her about what you hope she will gain from dating.

2. "Who is the 'dream guy'?" Have fun creating a list of the attributes she is looking for in a guy. You can challenge her to make a list of attributes she will want to embody so she can attract a great guy too!

3. "Should we (the parents) meet your date? If so, when?" This question will give you some insight into what she is

thinking about relationships too. You can share with her your expectations at an early age so she is aware when she does become interested in boys.

4. "What is needed to stay pure?" This question touched on many topics such as guarding your heart, guarding your eyes, respecting yourself and your future husband, being smart, and creating accountability. Think through what aspects you want to focus on. This may be a series of smaller conversations that come up naturally or as part of a special weekend away.

Conversation 7

• • •

THE MONEY TALK

Understanding Dollars and Sense

One thing is universal: Tweens love to have and spend money! How can we as parents help our daughters learn the value of money?

Ten-year-old Jade had four dollars to spend and wanted desperately to buy a toy her mother knew was not a good choice. Mom cautioned her daughter, "Jade, is this really a wise purchase? It looks like it would easily break." Ignoring her mom's advice, she bought it anyway.

Mom: "Would you believe it broke before she got to the car. On the ride home I heard Jade, who was in the backseat, say, 'Mom, you were right! I should have listened.' Four dollars for a toy that broke may well be worth the lesson she learned through experience."

Maybe next time Jade will listen to Mom—or not!

"Where Does Your Money Come From Now?"

After hearing, "We can't buy that because it costs too much money," a five-year-old girl told her mother they should simply "Go to that machine by the bank and get more money out." If only it were that easy! What a great representation of the misunderstandings young people often have about money and how it is earned.

Your daughter probably has a pretty good sense of where her spending money currently comes from. Does she get an allowance, or do you give her money whenever she asks? Does she earn her money by doing certain chores or baby-sitting? Maybe she gets cash from grandparents for birthdays or holidays.

Personal spending money doesn't seem to matter that much to most young children under the age of nine or ten. But something happens as the tween brain begins to notice fashion and become more social. It takes significantly more money to meet your friends at the mall, go shopping, see movies, and eat out. Your tween daughter is now recognizing that more money in her pocket means more opportunities to go places, do things with her friends, and buy the things she wants. As these activities increase, so do the requests for money. It can be exhausting (and expensive) for parents! But these growing requests for spending cash also present an opportunity to teach your daughter important concepts about budgeting, saving, and setting goals.

Most kids don't have a great understanding of how much things cost. Their inexperience with money means they have no scale to judge things against. They don't know if a house costs $5,000 or $500,000; they don't understand that a new car can easily be priced over $20,000; and they likely have no idea of your household income. Until they start handling money themselves, they can't really appreciate how it works.

We (the Larsons) found that our twelve-year-old began to understand money when she began to earn it through her baby-sitting jobs. Before this time, the only money she ever had was the money she was given. She would spend it on silly things, lose it, or give it away with almost no concept of its value. But when Kate began to earn her own money, she began to make better decisions, set some goals, and save up for the things she wanted.

The healthy shift that is needed is for the parent to move from "I earn and control all the money" to "You begin to earn some money and learn how to handle it." Your tween can start earning some of her own money by doing chores around the house, baby-sitting younger kids in the neighborhood, or even setting up a lemonade stand. It is healthy for her to see what goes into earning money, and this understanding will definitely affect the way she spends.

We also wanted to avoid the constant requests for more cash. It was ten dollars for a movie, twenty dollars for a trip with friends to the mall, forty dollars for that shirt I must have . . . it never ended! We decided to increase the kids' allowance and give it to them once a month. The catch was this is all they would get. We would cover basics (like shoes and essential clothing needs), but they would need to budget for all activities or extras. If they wanted fancier shoes than we were willing to buy, it was out of their budget. Movies, five-dollar smoothies, makeup, and trips to the mall with friends would need to come out of their

---

ARP *Adage*

Tweens would rather learn by experience than from the ex-perienced—especially when it comes to money! Wise parents look for ways to allow their child to experience natural consequences.

own monthly budget. If they didn't think they had enough, they could earn more by finding odd jobs or other creative ways to supplement their income.

When we went to this flat-rate monthly allowance system, Kate became more serious about getting baby-sitting jobs; our son found a way to get paid to take care of the neighbor's two dogs; and our youngest, Anna, helped build a lemonade stand on wheels and regularly runs successful lemonade sales in the neighborhood. It is gratifying to see all three of them thinking and acting more responsible in the area of finances. It is also nice to avoid the role of parental ATM for the nearly daily requests that begin to emerge in the tween years.

"What Things Do You Currently Need Money For?"

The 2014 annual report from the investment firm Piper Jaffray looked at how teens are currently spending their money. For the first time, teens are now spending as much on food as they are on clothing. The breakdown looks something like this: 21 percent on food and drink (with Starbucks at the top of the list), 21 percent on clothing, 10 percent on accessories/personal care, 8 percent on car, 8 percent on shoes, 8 percent on electronics, 7 percent on video games, 6 percent on movies, 6 percent on events, and the remaining 5 percent on miscellaneous items.

We definitely saw this shift as our tweens wanted more and more to spend money at Starbucks. Tweens and teens are currently very into the Starbucks brand and love to order off the "secret menu" and post pictures of themselves on social media holding their favorite Starbucks concoctions. Walking into school with a Starbucks is somewhat of a status thing. These requests for five-dollar specialty drinks was part of what drove us to move toward an allowance system that empowers the kids to spend their own money, even if it means they blow it all on what Mom and Dad think are overpriced and silly beverages.

It is especially easy to spend somebody else's money. I (Peter) remember taking a six-month trip abroad in college and my dad let me take his credit card "in case of an emergency." It was so easy and convenient to take out that little plastic card and charge those small extras (which added up to a big total). It started with a couple gifts for family, and then went to better food from nicer restaurants, and finally escalated to staying the weekend in an upscale hotel because I was so sick of the rundown dorms in which we'd been stuck for months. None of these things was an "emergency," but it was just so easy to spend *Dad's* money.

Somehow my financial personality completely shifted when it was no longer Dad's money. When it is my own hard-earned money, I'm typically very frugal and conservative. In the twenty years Heather and I have been married, I've never been considered a big spender. We've seen a noticeable shift for many kids once they begin to earn their own money and set some goals for things they want to buy.

As you answer this question, think about the things you're willing to cover simply because you love and want to provide for your children. But also take time to think about the things your daughter could begin to buy for herself. How can you help her understand more of what it means to make good financial decisions?

"When Will You Need to Pay for Expenses Related to a Car, Smartphone, Clothes, Food, or Entertainment?"

As culture changes and technology advances, there are ever-increasing demands for the latest and greatest devices. According to a recent study, 70 percent of teens between thirteen and seventeen now own a smartphone. That's up from 58 percent in 2012 and 36 percent in 2011.[1] By the time this book is printed, the 70 percent figure will be a very low estimate. The most popular smartphones can cost over five hundred dollars and always come with a monthly bill to cover the talk, text, and data demands of the device. Who pays for all of this?

Most teens are excited to get their driver's license, and you can count on getting the question, "Can I have a car?" With the driver's license comes the need to insure a teen driver in your home, and with the car comes ongoing gas and maintenance. Nationwide insurance surveyed almost fifteen hundred parents adding a teen driver to their policy and found the average increase was eight hundred dollars per year. Are you ready for this? Have you and your spouse discussed what your plan will be?

At what age should a child begin to gain access to the privilege of a smartphone or car? It may be a good idea to underline that word *privilege*, as these items truly are privileges to own. But with privilege comes responsibility. Circle the word *responsibility* and draw a line back to *privilege*. These two concepts are highly connected. There was a time when one earned privileges by showing themselves to be responsible. How you drive a car and use a phone are huge opportunities to prove yourself responsible. But as we mention in "The Tech Talk" chapter that follows, our culture now gives kids all sorts of privileges with almost no expectations of responsibility.

There is not one right answer for every family. Depending on your resources, your own past experiences, and your child's personality, your answer to the question of when your daughter should begin to pay for some of her own expenses will vary. When it comes to paying for these items, it will range from *nothing* to *everything* paid by the parents. The less you're willing to cover, the more likely the topic of getting a job will come up. Are you clear on when and if you'd like your tween/teen to get a job?

Being on the same page as parents and clearly communicating these expectations to your tween early on is important. The further the distance between expectations and reality, the more disappointment and frustration she will experience when reality hits.

"What Are the Financial Plans/Expectations for After High School or College?"

Heather and I (Peter) grew up in very different homes. As she and her brothers left for college, her parents clearly informed each child they would have support for four years of college. At the end of the fourth year, whether they were finished with their studies or not, they would be cut off from all financial support. This meant no more help with a car, no moving back home, and no money when you get into a pinch. They had been informed (with four years' advance notice) to prepare to support themselves. Her parents followed through on this plan, and each kid stepped up to the plate to fully support him or herself right out of college. They made sure they finished their majors, lined up jobs or internships, and had saved up for a reliable car for transportation.

My father, on the other hand, was generous and accommodating. He was always there as a safety net to provide a second chance. He allowed my three older brothers and me to try many educational programs, live at home as long as needed, and provided financial help whenever we needed. As a result, it took many years for each boy to find true independence apart from the support of Dad. His generous support became a crutch that made it harder to launch. I was ten years younger than my oldest brother and began to notice this trend as I grew up. At some point, I realized I actually needed to cut my father off from supporting me any longer if I would ever learn to stand on my own. Admittedly, that is a little backwards and somewhat extreme compared to most young adults' experience. But loving, well-intentioned parents are everywhere; it is easy to overindulge our daughters without even recognizing it.

You'll need to decide what is the right amount of support for your children, but do them the favor of letting them know what to expect. While it might seem early to discuss some of these topics, the four short years from eighth grade to graduation will move faster than you think. Another key is to make sure you get on the same page as parents. This may take a while, especially if you come from very different home environments. Discussing these questions as a couple will help you prepare for the conversations you'll have with your daughter later on.

- What happens if she doesn't go to college? How much support is there after high school?

- Do you expect her to hold a part-time job while in college?

- How much of her own education, books, and room and board should she expect to pay for while in college?

- Can your adult daughter move back home if needed? For how long?

- How will you handle health insurance, student loan debt, car insurance, etc., after college?

- In the long run, which is more loving: providing unending financial support, or cutting her off at some point?

- How did your parents handle financial support after high school and college? What would you like to repeat or not repeat with your children?

"If You Were Given $500 Right Now, What Would You Do With It?"

A great way to end this conversation is with this very fun question about how she would handle an unexpected gift of cash. Not only is it enlightening to hear her dreams, but the answers can be very telling as well. There are three main things we listen for as we've heard our girls answer this question.

Spenders vs Savers

First, most individuals naturally fall into one of two categories: *spenders* or *savers*. Savers tend to view money as a source of security and don't like to wonder if they have enough to cover their expenses. If your daughter is a natural saver, you might hear her talk about buying one or two small things and tucking the rest into a savings account or her piggy bank. She may already have a goal she is saving up for, and this cash would go toward that special experience or item she has in mind for the future. Spenders, on the other hand, view money as a source of enjoyment. They may live more in the moment and love to experience things today. Money just tends to "burn a hole in their pocket." They are often willing to pay for others to share in their joy as well. Why wait if you can have it today? Why do it alone if you can share with others?

Either approach—spender or saver—can get out of balance if not monitored. It is good to begin to understand what type of financial personality your daughter has so you can help her avoid the pitfalls of becoming too extreme in either direction. Spenders can quickly dig themselves a hole as they make quick or poor decisions with their money. One passage from the Old Testament of the Bible says, "Whoever loves money never has enough money; whoever loves wealth is never satisfied with their income" (Ecclesiastes 5:10). Spenders often feel like they never have enough money. They tend to live in a state of confusion and stress around money, wondering where it all goes.

Savers have their own pitfalls, yearning for a false security through money and missing out on the experiences life has to offer. Matthew 6:21 reminds us, "For where your treasure is, there your heart will be also." Truer words were never spoken; savers need to guard against this miserly notion of always trying to store up treasure for tomorrow. The more she saves, the more her heart can become consumed by it, never leading to a sense of contentment. Don't feel like you need to address all of this spender or saver talk today; this question will simply help you understand your daughter better as you anticipate future challenges she could face.

Spend, Save, Give

A second key topic this question invites is the discussion around how income is allocated in terms of spending, saving, and giving. Depending on your family's values and beliefs, you may have some strong opinions about giving a certain percent to church, charities, or nonprofit organizations. It is never too early to begin teaching and modeling a generous approach to giving and sharing the wealth with which you are blessed.

> Command those who are rich in this present world not to be arrogant nor to put their hope in wealth, which is so uncertain, but to put their hope in God, who richly provides us with everything for our enjoyment. Command them to do good, to be rich in good deeds, and to be generous and willing to share.
>
> 1 Timothy 6:17–18

An early discussion around how to allocate income between saving, spending, and giving can have a dramatic and lasting impact on your daughter. I've met adults in midlife who give away 10 percent, save 20 percent, and spend the remaining 70 percent. They often reference an early conversation with a parent who instructed them accordingly. By adopting this approach early, they've learned to live generously and within their means. This is super important as we live in a culture where 25 percent of American adults have no savings at all, and the average credit card debt is over two thousand dollars.[2]

Conversation Idea

Tell your daughter you only have ten dollars to spend on a special parent-daughter date (between the two of you). Let her pick the place and see if the two of you can stick to the budget while you have this conversation about money.

1. "Where does your money come from?" This is a simple conversation starter.

2. "What things do you currently need money for?" Find out what your daughter thinks she needs to spend her money on today.

3. "When will you need to pay for expenses related to a car, smartphone, clothes, food, or entertainment?" After talking with your spouse, ask your daughter what her expectations for these might be. Share with her your thoughts and expectations as well.

4. "What are the financial plans/expectations for after high school or college?" Although this seems light-years away, setting clear expectations at a young age will be a benefit in the future.

5. "If you were given $500 right now, what would you do with it?" Oh, what a fun question to explore with your tween. Share your thoughts too!

Online Resources
www.kidsinthehouse.com
www.themint.org

Conversation 8

• • •

THE TECH TALK

*Rights, Responsibilities, Privileges
(and Screens)*

Rachel Canning of Morristown, New Jersey, made national headlines a few years ago as she sued her parents for "financially abandoning" her at age eighteen. Her lawsuit demanded that her parents pay her college tuition, a request they were refusing. Her father had a different take on the situation and reported that she had run away from home after failing to follow simple household rules involving chores and a curfew. After a few weeks, Rachel dropped the lawsuit and returned home, but her story raises questions about rights, responsibilities, and privileges in a culture of entitlement.

Many tweens and teens assume certain privileges will be their right: "When I'm twelve I'll get a smartphone." These tweens can appear to be demanding and entitled instead of grateful.

But some adults also get confused about rights versus privileges, and assume their daughter should have access to every privilege possible. The issue is further confused by a culture that says giving our kids the very best is generous and loving, with little consideration of when this generosity becomes indulgent or misguided. Most parents agree there are basic rights they are responsible for providing: food, shelter, safety, education, health care, and so on. The rights on this list are actually necessary for the healthy development of children.

It gets fuzzy, however, when your eleven-year-old daughter wants the latest tablet computer and an Instagram account so she can follow her friends digitally. Privileges go beyond rights and involve things that are desirable but not necessary for healthy development. Privileges include things like a smart-phone, a Facebook account, or permission to drive the car. Privileges such as these can be earned. Sometimes that means your daughter earns the money to purchase things herself, and other times it means she demonstrates an appropriate level of responsibility to be rewarded with a new privilege. And just as privileges can be earned, they can also be lost!

Your tween has many roles in her life. She is a daughter, student, friend, classmate, and likely a sister, neighbor, or teammate. With each role she has in life, there are basic responsibilities to go along with it. It is important for your daughter to understand the expectations associated with these different roles. As parents, we have a standard set of responsibilities we expect from our daughters. We expect our tween daughters to listen to us, be respectful, and help out around the house. As a student, we expect her to be responsible by working hard in school, getting along with her teachers and other classmates, and learning grade-appropriate material. Conscious or not, we judge our tween's behavior against these expectations, and there are consequences and rewards based on whether or not she fulfills her responsibilities. If she fails to live up to the expectations, there are usually consequences. Sometimes the consequences are natural (she gets a poor grade because she did not study), and other times the consequences are imposed by parents (she's grounded or loses her smartphone for a week). If she meets or exceeds expectations (she makes the National Honor Society), there may be rewards or privileges granted (she gets to stay out an hour later with her friends).

Help your daughter understand that these roles and responsibilities are not something you're assigning, but rather simple observations about how life works. It is as true for an adult as it is for a child. As adults, we have roles and an associated set of responsibilities with being a parent, spouse, employee, etc. Like our children, we experiences rewards and consequences in life based on how others judge our behavior against these role-based expectations. If you do a great job at work, perhaps you get that promotion or bonus. If you are rude to others, friends keep their distance.

One important job of parenting is to be clear with your daughter about the basic responsibilities you expect of her in her varying roles, such as daughter, sister, friend, student, teammate, musician. If she is part of extracurricular activities such as sports or music lessons, define her basic responsibilities around each of these commitments. Maturity and responsibility are displayed when these basic expectations are met consistently and independently, creating room for more privileges. If these responsibilities begin to slip, natural consequences or loss of privilege will be the result.

For the remainder of the chapter we will look at questions to help you determine your stance regarding a number of technology privilege requests that typically emerge during the teen years. While these issues involve common topics (smartphones, social media, and entertainment), they can create confusion and cause challenges for parents. We don't want to dictate the right answer on each of these topics for your family, and this is not a one-size-fits-all approach. Instead, we will process two questions designed to help you discern the best approach for your daughter (and family).

In the context of a specific girl's story, we'll explore answers adopted by other parents for their situations. Note that the list of topics is not comprehensive, as it mainly focuses on technology questions girls are asking. There are sure to be additional topics you need to tackle on your own, but these same principles apply.

For each of the topics listed, we suggest you define your answers to two basic questions. First, "What are the added responsibilities associated with this privilege?" Consider the following issues when answering this question:

- Make sure you've made the expectations both clear and reasonable.

- Make sure, as parents, you're both on the same page. Be consistent in terms of what you communicate about expected responsibilities. Don't undermine one another and thereby confuse your daughter.

- As you consider the increased responsibilities (and risks) associated with this privilege, make sure your daughter is developmentally ready to manage it. If you determine she's not ready, it is acceptable to say, "No, not yet."

The second question is "What are the consequences and rewards when this privilege is abused or used correctly?" As you answer, consider the following:

- Just like expectations, make sure the consequences and rewards are clearly communicated to your daughter.

- Be consistent! If you clearly communicate an expectation and associated consequence or reward, you need to follow through on what you've said. Otherwise you quickly become irrelevant as a parent.

- Sometimes there are natural consequences. That is even better, since then you don't have to be the bad guy. Instead, you can empathize and support her as she encounters important lessons. Don't rescue her so quickly that she fails to learn the lesson life is teaching.

- Keep in mind the very fact that something referred to as a "privilege" means it is a reward in itself to keep exercising that privilege.

"When Do I Get a Smartphone?"

This is a burning question for many tweens. Given the number of tweens who posses a phone, your daughter may be convinced it is a *right* and not a *privilege*. It is our opinion, however, that this falls clearly in the privilege category. Consider that you yourself survived your tween years without a smartphone. Your daughter may already own a phone, so your process may be more about how to keep this privilege moving in a positive direction.

Amanda, age twelve, is the youngest of three and could not wait to get a smartphone like her older siblings. A typical tween, she played on a soccer team but often felt out of the loop since she was not part of the group texts that floated around amongst her friends. Finally, her parents added a line to their family plan and bought her a smartphone for Christmas. Amanda immediately felt more connected and fashionable because she had the latest and greatest device in her back pocket. She expected to text her friends many times per day, download and play games, post awesome selfies to her newly created social media accounts, and listen to music whenever she wanted. Her parents, however, had a completely different set of expectations.

What are the added responsibilities associated with this privilege?

Amanda's parents believe that owning a powerful and expensive piece of technology, such as a smartphone, should provide an increased level of freedom and autonomy along with the responsibility to stay in communication through phone calls and texts. As parents, they expect her to use the smartphone to keep them informed of where she is and what her plans are. They expect her to pick up when they call, and they expect her to keep track of her phone and not treat it recklessly in a way that could break it.

In order to maintain communication with Amanda, her parents expect she will have her phone charged, especially when she is heading out to situations where they need to get ahold of her, such as soccer practices or trips to the mall with her friends. Her mother and father expect her to turn the phone off during class or dinner and pay attention to what is happening around her. To help her get sleep at night, they expect her to keep her phone in a central location, outside of her bedroom, after a certain time of night. The phone should also be kept in this location during study time so she can stay focused and complete her homework.

Amanda's family spent quite a bit of time together in the car. After she and her siblings each had a smartphone, her mother noticed how their family conversations went from lively to nonexistent in the car. Playing games and checking social media was taking away from conversation and observation of the world around them. They decided that using the phone to communicate with someone else (text or call) was okay in the car, but no games. This change brought balance back to their car time. (Obviously, once the kids become drivers, there will need to be a new set of rules around texting and talking in the car.) Amanda's parents expect she will communicate digitally with her friends in the same mature, friendly way she does in her face-to-face communication. They will not allow her to perpetuate lies, spread negative messages about others, or threaten or bully anyone. They want her to continue to be a respectable and responsible friend in the digital world, just as she is in real life. In order to maintain this healthy type of communication, they created a rule stating that they will have knowledge of her current passwords at all times. They make it clear that, as parents, they have the right to look through her past texts or social media posts to ensure safe and respectful communication is ongoing.

As a parent, stay firm—you have a right to access your daughter's phone or computer. A word of caution, though: Don't abuse this right by constantly or secretly checking her texts. Respecting her privacy is a step of trust, and she will be more open in sharing her passwords if she realizes why the rule is in place and how you plan to use this access.

What are the consequences and rewards when the smartphone is abused or used correctly?

Remember, agreeing on the outcomes (consequences and rewards) and following through is just as important as setting clear expectations. Amanda's parents have settled on the following consequences and rewards regarding the expectations for owning a smartphone:

- If the phone is broken, damaged, or lost, Amanda will have to pay for the replacement or deal with the natural consequences of a cracked screen. If she takes good care of the phone, she will have the enjoyment of a well-working device.

- If she lets the phone battery die when she leaves the house, or puts it on mute and does not respond to calls or texts from her parents, she will lose the phone for one to five days, depending on the situation. If she keeps the phone well charged, has the ringer on, answers when her parents call or text, and uses the phone to notify them of changes in her plans, they will continue to pay for her line and let her use the phone for other more enjoyable activities including games and music.

- If Amanda is checking her phone during family dinner, gets in trouble for using her phone during class, or sneaks it into her room at night, she will lose it for several days, depending on the situation. If, on the other hand, she keeps it on the central charging station at night, puts it on mute during dinner and class, and doesn't use it constantly in the car, she can continue to have the privilege of using the phone. Her parents might even buy her that new case she wants for it.

- When Amanda uses her phone for safe and respectful communication by checking in regularly with her parents, keeping up with her grandparents, and coordinating activities with her friends, she is praised and encouraged to keep it up. If her parents find she is using her phone to exclude friends (ignoring texts from friends), they'll call her out. If she is not being a good friend, there will be natural consequences from those friends, but there may need to be more imposed consequences as well, such as apologizing to others or losing her phone for a period of time.

On one occasion, Amanda had just gotten her new phone and asked her mom if she could go to the nearby convenience store with her friends. Amanda's mom agreed to let her go and reminded her to be home by five for dinner and an evening church service. At 5:10 Amanda wasn't home, so her mother began calling (no answer) and texting, "How close are you?" No response. Another text at 5:20: "Dinner is ready, where are you?" No response. Her mother tried calling again and it went directly to voicemail. She could tell Amanda had turned off the phone! When Amanda finally returned home at six, her mom had left for church and her dad was there to talk through the consequences of not only breaking a curfew, but also not using her cell phone as the communication device it was intended to be. Amanda made some poor excuses about not picking up in front of her friends, but in the end had her phone taken away for a week as she learned the importance of responding promptly when called or texted by her parents.

When you determine your daughter's behavior to be responsible, you allow her to keep using the phone as needed and gladly pay the monthly bill to have her on your data, text, and cellular plan. It almost becomes a nonissue when expectations are being met. The guidelines like the ones described above will help your daughter embrace privileges with increasing responsibility. You can't control her, but you can maximize your influence by being clear, reasonable, and consistent.

Being a good friend in person requires knowing when to step out of conversations that are negative or hurtful about others. With group texts, girls will need to know how to exit a conversation if it has become negative. Sometimes, the content of the text isn't an issue but the sheer number of texts can become overwhelming. Helping your daughter talk through strategies of how to exit these conversations gracefully will become a lifelong skill. Technology and instant communication is only on the increase!

Remember, the end goal for your daughter is to learn how to be a good friend and act with integrity—whether in person or via text, social media, or some other avenue in the future. And empowering her to manage her smartphone use is an important evolution. As she shows signs of maturity, you'll want to increase her control. After all, you can't be in her college dorm room trying to influence her smartphone use.

"How Will Social Media Be Used in Our Home?"

Long gone is the world in which you came home from school and connected with friends in person or over the landline. Now a girl's social network is with her constantly on computers, tablets, and in her back pocket on her smartphone. There is no escape; it is a constant force in her life. There are ever increasing forms of social and digital communication bombarding our teens. The Facebook of yesterday has become the Instagram and Snapchat of today. Who knows what it will be tomorrow (when you're reading this book). Keeping up with the specific social media channels in which your daughter is connecting with her friends is not easy, but it is important.

Consider Emma, who wanted to get her first smartphone at age eleven. On the bus to and from school, she would sit with her friends as they posted pictures and reviewed their Instagram accounts. This was the one thing Emma was most excited about. She so wanted to create an Instagram account and share pictures and posts with her friends, to see how many "followers" and "likes" she could get. She was beginning to notice that the most popular kids had the most *followers* and always received the most *likes* when they posted something. While intriguing, it was also a little scary to see this quantified definition of popularity so clearly displayed.

What are the added responsibilities associated with this privilege?

As Emma made her intentions clear to her parents, they felt it was important to sit down for a discussion and clarify their expectations.

Social networks leverage the idea of connecting, following, and "friending" other people on the network. Kids often equate a higher number of connections with some sort of status. Because of this, it is not uncommon to friend and follow anyone and everyone. Tween girls need to realize, however, the importance of connecting only with people you know. It is possible for people with bad intentions to pose as someone else in order to develop trust. Emma's parents told her the story of a man in his forties who was pretending to be a junior high girl on a social network. Once he became an online friend with these girls, he was asking them to behave inappropriately. Luckily, he was caught. But not all stories end this well. By setting the expectation of connecting only with people she knew, Emma's parents increased her safety.

They also informed her she was never to plan on meeting someone in person that she had met online. They let her know how dangerous this can be. They took the opportunity to tell her this applied to any digital relationship, including participants in online games or apps, not only the social networks in which she participated.

Another responsibility associated with social media is not sharing passwords with anyone, even friends. Emma's parents warned her about sharing her password. Some kids will log in and pretend to be posting as someone else. The friends may think this is funny or a joke, but it can be hurtful and damage relationships or reputations.

Emma's parents expected her to use common sense when she posted things to her account. Posts should be appropriate, respectful of others, and meet the "Grandma Rule." They explained the Grandma Rule meant that if she wouldn't be comfortable sharing it with her grandmother, she shouldn't post it to social media. While simple, these guidelines actually protect against more serious issues such as sexting or online bullying.

Finally, Emma's parents informed her that they needed to be connected as friends on her social network. This would allow them the ability to follow her online activity and ensure her safety. Emma's parents had also learned from experience with her older siblings that kids will sometimes create alternative accounts without informing their parents. They will observe to see if she has little or no activity in her account, which is a tip that she may have created a new account without telling them.

What are the consequences and rewards when social media is abused or used correctly?

Emma's folks kept the consequences pretty clear and simple: Depending on the infraction, she would either need to shut down her account and/or lose her smartphone for a period of time.

- Minor issues would involve a day or two off her Instagram account.

- More serious issues would involve a week or more of losing her phone and staying out of her account.

- Serious safety concerns meant she would completely lose the privilege of having a social media account and using a smartphone until she was older and demonstrated more responsibility. Instead, they would replace her smartphone with a "dumb phone" (which had no Internet, data, or text plan) to be used for cell calls only.

Since having a social media account was determined to be a privilege in itself, they agreed the reward for responsible behavior would be the ability to keep using Instagram and perhaps create other accounts on additional social networks in the future.

"What Movies Can I Watch? What Songs Can I Download?"

Meet Sara, an eleven-year-old fifth-grader who is convinced her parents are "the worst" because they won't let her watch

PG-13 movies. She insists all of her friends get to watch them, and some have even seen R-rated movies. Even worse, they won't let her download or stream the most popular hip-hop songs. She keeps asking, begging, and complaining, but so far she's had no luck convincing her parents to change their minds.

Sara's mom is not crazy about television, movies, or pop music. She admits she is rather conservative and would prefer Sara not be exposed to any of this media. The more she looks into the content and themes of this music and the films, the less impressed she is. For these reasons, she is completely convinced these requests are privileges to be earned later, when Sara is older and more mature. Sara's mom is saying no for now.

What are the added responsibilities associated with this privilege?

Because Sara's parents are not allowing her requested privileges at this time, the nature of this question shifts to something more like "What responsibilities must Sara demonstrate in order to earn the privileges she wants?" As they discussed their decision, they clarified several things they expect.

First, they expect her to stop fussing and complaining, and to respect their decision. They have told her she can begin watching PG-13 movies when she turns thirteen. It is their belief that these ratings are there for a reason. In terms of music, they expect her to seek permission before she downloads new songs. Her mother will use an online resource, such as www.commonsensemedia.org or www.pluggedin.com, to review the music Sara is requesting and let her know what she can and cannot buy. Her mother has extended this rule to books as well, noticing that teen novels are becoming increasingly popular and sophisticated.

ARP *Adage*

Sometimes the best response is to answer a question with another question, like "What do you think makes the most sense?" or "What are the options?" Questions like these will encourage your daughter to think on her own and to come to better conclusions.

In the end, they want Sara to demonstrate the maturity to have thoughtful conversations about the stories being told, the themes being presented, the choices being made in these forms of media. They want her to have a chance to define and establish her own moral compass before Hollywood inserts its powerful influence.

Consider one smart technique shared by a twelve-year-old girl. "My mom has this wonderful way of getting through. She doesn't say, 'You should' when I need help with a decision, but 'Have you considered . . . ?' or 'Maybe this would work . . .' giving me the final choice. And she lets me rattle on with just enough encouragement until I sort things out."

What are the consequences and rewards when this privilege is abused or used correctly by Sara?

- If Sara can respect their decision and honor these boundaries, she will earn their trust and the privilege to consume more sophisticated media as she matures.

- If she does not follow these guidelines, she will lose the privilege of watching any movies or listening to music with her friends. Her parents agreed to start by enforcing these consequences for a week if she is caught breaking the rules. They will extend to multiple weeks if the irresponsible behavior continues.

We (the Larsons) attended a conference in 2012 and heard some powerful thoughts about parenting. Dr. Pat Love was giving a plenary address for the National Association of Relationship and Marriage Education (NARME). Her overarching point was that parents need to "make adulthood look attractive to young people." As she unpacked this premise, she talked about the relationship between responsibilities and privileges. Traditionally, one earns more privileges as one grows up and demonstrates increasing responsibility. You earn the privilege of driving a car by demonstrating the knowledge and skill needed to pass the driver's exam. Or, you get to drive when you have a part-time job and can help contribute to gas and insurance bills.

But our Western culture has begun to turn this around. The knee-jerk reaction is to say yes to everything. We give kids all sorts of privileges and none of the responsibility. Kids get to go where adults go, use the same powerful technology, drive nice cars, wear expensive fashionable clothes, and have access to an endless stream of entertainment. If we say yes to everything a child wants, what incentive is there to grow up? Why would I want to get a job and move out of the house someday if I get every privilege an adult has now and nothing is expected of me?

One option is to say no sometimes. "No, you can't join us for dinner tonight. We are going out for a date." "No, you can't get your driver's license until you find a part-time job and can help pay for gas." "No, I'm not buying you the latest smartphone." The premise is adults should have things and do things that

---

ARP *Adage*

Remember, when dealing with any major issue, your influence as the parent is directly related to the relationship you have with your adolescent.

kids can't until kids begin to grow up and earn those privileges for themselves. Make adulthood look like something to aspire toward. Occasionally your daughter should be saying, "I can't wait until I grow up so I can . . ."

Remember to make adulthood look attractive. There may be certain decisions you make that she doesn't like. That's okay. You're sure to hear the old pleas for equity as she bargains against what her friends or older siblings get, but don't cave too quickly. If everything comes easily, we don't learn hard work and responsibility. Over time, she'll take great pride and satisfaction in earning privileges and demonstrating a mature level of responsibility. A new type of comparison will start to emerge as she notices the lack of responsibility (and gratitude) in her peers.

1. "When do I get a smartphone?" You may hesitate to bring up this question if it's not already being asked in your home. Be sure, the question is coming! Talking with your tween may end unnecessary begging in the future.

2. "How will social media be used in our home?" Find out what social media your daughter is thinking about. Talk about the responsibilities associated with social media and your expectations.

3. "What movies can I watch? What songs can I download?" This question provides opportunity to hear what songs and movies your daughter is interested in. Take time to explore her music, and talk about what you hear together.

(Additional questions for each topic)

What are the added responsibilities associated with this privilege?

What are the consequences and rewards when this privilege is abused or used correctly?

BONUS ACTIVITIES

Project Thirteen and Birthday Boxes

We hope you have enjoyed your conversations with your daughter. The end of the tween years is only the beginning of the teenage years. Soon your daughter will be thirteen, and in five short years she will be eighteen, which is old enough to vote and the age when many kids leave home for college, the military, or the job market.

The onset of the teen years comes with insecurities and fears for both parents and adolescent. Most tweens long for their parents to acknowledge that they are growing up and therefore shouldn't treat them "like little kids." For good reasons, many cultures provide a rite of passage into adolescence. She's going through a huge developmental transition and needs reassurance and the recognition that she can make it. Providing adequate structure will help her feel safe, in control of her life, and prepared for the future. To help with that pursuit, we want to suggest two practical projects that helped us and many other parents successfully launch our teenagers into the world of adulthood. Both of these activities are adapted from David and Claudia Arp's book *Suddenly They're 13.*[1]

One is Project Thirteen, a planned one-time challenge to help your daughter prepare for the teen years. Another is a plan of release we call Birthday Boxes, which help hand off new responsibilities and privileges so that by the time she's eighteen, your daughter is equipped to function on her own as an adult. First, let's look at Project Thirteen.

Project Thirteen

Julia, the mom of a twelve-year-old girl, exclaimed, "Adolescence is such a scary time to even think about letting go. Plus, I already feel like I'm losing control!"

"You are losing control," I (Claudia) told her. "That's what it's all about. But you want to lose control in a controlled manner!"

Today, as you look at your daughter, as scary as it may be, you are going to lose control whether you plan for it or not, so what can you do to get this process started on a positive note?

Fortunately, kids come programmed for independence. Their job is to break away and become autonomous people. Communicate to your daughter that a day is coming when she will grow up and leave your home, and a significant part of your job, as the parent, is to help facilitate this process. When she realizes you are aware that she is maturing and growing up, she might be much more cooperative.

So let us share with you a strategy for launching kids into the teenage years, which was shared with us years ago by our friends Paul and Phyllis Stanley. Project Thirteen is a rite of passage that will help your daughter enter the teen years a little less shaky, a little more self-assured, and a little more positive.

And as the parent, you can embrace this new phase of family life with real hope instead of a sense of impending doom.

Designing the Project

Several months before your daughter's thirteenth birthday, present the idea of Project Thirteen and together decide what to include in the challenge. Relay to your daughter something like this: "We're excited that in a few months you are going to be a teenager. We are entering a new phase of family life. No longer will we relate to you as a child. Actually, you are becoming a 'pre-adult,' and we want to build a more adult relationship with you. We want to help you prepare for your teen years by giving you a one-time project that we call Project Thirteen."

Then explain the project, which includes goals in four different areas: physical, intellectual, spiritual, and practical. For motivation, tell your daughter, "If you complete it by your thirteenth birthday, you will receive a reward."

After explaining the concept, you could say something like, "I'd like you to think about how you would like to grow in each of these areas. Brainstorm specific projects or activities you could do in these areas. Then we'll sit down together and write the project."

Along with this proposal is an important message: "We are excited! (instead of scared and anxious!) You are getting ready to enter a special time of life. You're on your way to adulthood. We want to help you be ready for this new phase of your life, and this challenge will help you prepare. It is a big deal! You are going to be a teenager, and we are happy about this!"

Positive excitement is contagious, and hopefully you can infect your daughter with a positive attitude of anticipation and also give the gift of advance preparation.

Be creative. Customize the challenge to fit your daughter's individual needs and personality. If your daughter has difficulty handling money, you could challenge her to learn how to keep a budget. Or maybe she needs to learn some practical skills like cooking a meal, washing and folding her own laundry, or typing on a keyboard. Program the challenge for success by including tasks in areas in which your daughter is gifted, but also more difficult challenges, or else it will have little meaning. Here is a sample Project Thirteen:

Olivia's Project Thirteen

1. Physical Goals

   A. Run a mile in under eight minutes.

   B. Learn to play a good game of tennis: work on serve, forehand, and backhand.

2. Intellectual Goals

   A. Read a biography about someone you admire and give an oral report.

   B. Read one classic novel.

3. Spiritual Goals

   A. Decide what your own standards and convictions will be for your teenage years.

   B. Read the book of Proverbs (one chapter a day for a month). Write down a verse from each chapter and identify some helpful life principles.

4. Practical Goals

   A. Earn $50. Parents will match what you earn and save before your birthday.

   B. Plan and prepare a family dinner.

The timing can be flexible, but allowing enough time is essential. You need to find the time line that will work for you. If you give the challenge too far in advance, she might lose motivation to complete it. We would suggest two to three months before her birthday as a good time frame. One parent gave her daughter the challenge two weeks before her birthday; their house was in complete chaos for those fourteen days. A last-minute challenge is not recommended. Plan ahead.

When every item has been checked off the Project Thirteen list, it's time to celebrate. Here are several suggestions:

1. Give your daughter a gift for a job well done. It may be a surprise, or she may have suggested it. Maybe it's a special experience, trip, or item she's been hoping for. Some kids need more motivation than others, so it's smart to tie the challenge in with a gift they really want. Whatever the gift, the message is, "Congratulations on a job well done. We are proud of you!"

2. Celebrate! Choose your new teenager's favorite menu. Include family and friends in the celebration. Make your teenager the star for that day and tell others about her accomplishments!

A Challenge With a Big Payoff

After completing Project Thirteen, Michaela told her mom, "I like the fact that I really accomplished something." Another girl, Kirstin, commented, "In our class, only Joe (her Jewish friend who had completed his Bar Mitzvah) and I are really prepared to be teenagers!" At a time when so many kids feel insecure, you can give your daughter the gift of confidence through preparing for the coming teenage years. So when you reach this challenging stage of family life, turn it to your advantage by challenging your tween to get prepared for the

teenage years. Both you and your tween will reap many benefits in the years to come.

Steps for Creating Your Unique Project Thirteen

1. Explain Project Thirteen to your daughter, and give her a copy of the sample. Together discuss possible goals and projects. Ask your daughter to write down her own draft of the goals she would like to set.

2. Next, begin working on your version of her Project Thirteen. Consider your daughter's strengths and weaknesses. Choose positive areas you would like to reinforce, but also list the areas that you would like to strengthen.

3. Write specific goals for these areas: physical, intellectual, spiritual, and practical.

4. Evaluate your Project Thirteen by answering these questions:

   • Is it practical? Have I added too much or too little?

   • Is it programmed for success? Will it stretch my daughter, yet be obtainable?

   • Is it measurable? Will my daughter know when the requirements have been met? Is there a reasonable time limit?

   • Are the rewards clearly defined?

5. Make a date with your daughter for lunch or dinner. Compare the two lists and work together to combine them. Be sure to include items from your daughter's list, and don't force your ideas on her.

6. Discuss the reward. Would she like it to be a surprise? Or is there a special gift she would particularly like?

7. Together, agree on a final draft of her Project Thirteen, including a date by which the challenges should be completed.

But You Don't Know My Daughter

Will your almost-thirteen welcome a Project Thirteen? Two of our preteens thought it was cool, but one responded, "Do I really have to do this?" We chose a reward that was really appealing and encouraged our tween's participation.

What if your daughter is not cooperative? You're thinking, *She'll roll her eyes if I even suggest this!*

Know your daughter. Some children like the formality of a challenge that is well defined. Others think it's corny. One parent said, "I knew if I wanted my daughter to cooperate, I'd have to make it really low-key. With her, I never used the term *Project Thirteen,* but the summer before her thirteenth birthday I began to give her little pieces of it." Adapt this to fit your daughter's personality.

What If My Daughter Fails?

What if the initial excitement fizzles out? Not all kids or parents are great at follow-though. Here's how to salvage a half-completed challenge:

First, list all your daughter has already accomplished and give affirmation. Focus on what has been completed. If her challenge was unrealistic, simplify it. For instance, if her challenge included preparing meals for a week but it was impossible to meet this goal, modify that part of the challenge to cooking one three-course dinner for the family. Then talk together through the challenges yet to be met and modify them.

My Daughter Doesn't Need This

Some kids are super responsible, and a Project Thirteen might be boring. If you have a child like this, look for another rite of passage to help celebrate the entrance to the teenage years. One mom let her daughter completely redecorate her room. This was a real "letting go," since Mom was an interior decorator, and her daughter chose a color scheme of black and white. What about challenging your resistant daughter to complete a service project or to write her autobiography or philosophy of life?

Too Much Work?

Yes, this is work. Parenting is hard work every day. But the work involved in organizing, challenging, and supervising this rite of passage is worth it. Project Thirteen sets the stage for the coming teen years. Two benefits for the parents are

1. Establishing a positive and celebratory start to the teen years

2. Helping the family relate and support one another as a team

The benefits for the tween include

1. Beginning the teenage years with a sense of accomplishment

2. An increased awareness that her parents support her growing up

3. Developing comradeship with her parents and a realization that they are on one team

While the Project Thirteen isn't a cure-all for the stormy teenage years, it is a tool you can use to navigate the rough waters of transition from tween to teen. So be creative and intentional with your daughter, but most of all, have fun and keep it positive.

Countdown to Adulthood

After a successful launch into the teen years, the countdown to adulthood begins. Project Thirteen sets the stage for the coming teen years. This rite of passage gives your daughter a positive start and helps you begin to let go and to relate to your adolescent in a more mature way.

By completing this challenge, your daughter gains a sense of competence and accomplishment at a time in life typically filled with insecurities, and she begins to understand that you realize she is growing up and that you want to work together harmoniously to facilitate this process. Next, we want to tell you how to manage this process of release through the coming teenage years—how to lose control in a controlled way!

Remember, our job as parents is to work ourselves out of a job and into a relationship that will last for a lifetime. We wanted our sons to be able to function on their own before they left the nest at eighteen or nineteen years old, and we felt we needed a defined and targeted approach to releasing them into adulthood. So on each son's thirteenth birthday, we initiated an ongoing process of progressive release that we call the Arp Birthday Boxes.

The Birthday Box

Becoming a teenager at our house was a big deal. But after the family celebration, we planned another time to take our new teenager out to dinner with just the two of us. On this special occasion we tried to communicate the following message:

"We are excited about your growing up. You are now a teenager, and we want to relate to you on a more adult level. In five short years you will be eighteen and will probably be leaving for college. We want you to be prepared to make your own decisions, run your own life, and function as an adult. So, for the next five years, each year on your birthday we will give you new privileges and responsibilities for the coming year. This is progressive; our goal is that by the time you're eighteen, you will achieve adult status and be able to make your own choices."

Then we introduced the concept of the Arp Birthday Box and presented our new teenager with a small wooden box filled with cards. On each card was a new privilege or a new responsibility for the coming year. A typical thirteen-year-old birthday box might include areas like

1. Curfew

2. Academics

3. Smartphones, Screens, and Technology Privileges

4. Household Chores

5. Money

6. Social Life

7. Spiritual Life

While we didn't expect perfection with the Birthday Boxes, we did expect our teens to take them seriously and do their best. We gave them the following motivation: "If you manage your responsibilities well this year, then you'll move on to more privileges and responsibilities next year. Our goal is that you will be able to function as an adult by the time you leave home."

Then we gave each teen a projected plan of progression. We noted the progression across the page, which indicated independence at age eighteen. For each year we had new privileges and responsibilities illustrated in progressive boxes.

At that point, we discussed the coming year's box as well as the extended diagram. Nothing was in ink; all was negotiable. During this stage of life, we wanted our adolescent's input, and

AGE	13	14	15	16	17	18
CURFEW	10 p.m.	10:30	11:00	11:30	Midnight	None
ACADEMICS						
TECHNOLOGY						
HOUSEHOLD CHORES						
MONEY						
SOCIAL LIFE						
SPIRITUAL LIFE						

*Parents: Feel free to create a chart like the above for your own birthday box plan. The categories and curfew examples are only suggestions. As you complete your own chart, think about your daughter's unique style, goals, strengths, and growth areas.

we wanted to work together. So as our teens gave suggestions, we were willing to adapt our plan to the point all could buy in to it!

Warning! If the Birthday Box is only your input and your plan, don't expect your new teenager to jump up and down and go along with it. This is a cooperative effort! However, we did try to communicate the following:

"You can speed up this progression or slow it down. Basically, it's up to you how you manage your box. We don't think you're going to disappoint us. We're looking forward to watching you become a responsible adult."

How to Design a Teenage Birthday Box

First, you need an overall plan. However, the Birthday Box will be unique for each adolescent, as some teenagers are more responsible than others. Here are some areas to consider:

1. Curfew

We began at age thirteen with a curfew of 10:00 p.m. one night per weekend. In addition, we needed to know where the teen was going and whom he was going with. Each year we added thirty minutes to the curfew, so at age seventeen the curfew was midnight, and by eighteen he set his own curfew.

Many parents say their thirteen-year-olds really don't need a curfew as they are seldom out at night. Even so, it is helpful to establish the principle of the curfew before it is needed. Then extend the curfew each year. Your sixteen-year-old, whose curfew may be 11:30, does not feel as restricted because the curfew is thirty minutes later than when she was fifteen.

Our curfew was not an ironclad rule. We made exceptions for special events and school functions. Also, when a teen called to let us know he was running late, we willingly added a few minutes. (We avoided most late-night adventures, but not all!)

2. Academics/Homework

We began at age thirteen with limited supervision of homework and gradually worked toward their being totally responsible for their schoolwork. This was not the same age for each of our teens, because some took schoolwork more seriously. But by the time all of our sons were high school seniors, homework was their business, even if they got their priorities mixed up—and sometimes they did. They learned a valuable lesson in managing their time, a lesson that benefited them as freshmen in college. Since they had already experienced being on their own academically, they were able to handle the freedom of college life.

3. Screen Time

Putting tech (screens, Internet, social media, smartphone, and so on) in the Birthday Box can be a good way to teach responsible use and also can be a way for you to monitor your teen's progress. While we realize that technology has its inherent dangers, the solution is not in denying your daughter the benefits of these new tools. Technology is here to stay, so as a parent you need to help your daughter learn how to handle it in a responsible way. Some schools give assignments online and even require students to have a laptop or tablet. As scary as it is, it's up to you, the parent, to guide your daughter through the online maze. In designing your box, consider areas like the smartphone, gaming, surfing the Internet, Snapchat, Instagram, and whatever else is out there by the time this book is finished! Your goal is to have her learn to be totally responsible for her online life by age eighteen.

4. Household Chores

The Birthday Box will include responsibilities, not just privileges. Consider what you want your daughter to know about managing a household as she launches out on her own at eighteen years old. Is it reasonable to think she'll be able to cook, do her own laundry, clean the house, and take care of her things? Then build a progression into the Birthday Box. Perhaps it starts by keeping her own room clean. An occasional gift of a parent's helping hand will be appreciated, but sometimes it is better to close the door than to infringe on this agreement. Remember, this is a learning process.

In this area we have had very mixed results. One of our guys scored above average on housekeeping from the very beginning. Another lived in an unbelievable mess. Both finally got the picture: It's your responsibility, not ours. At least our boys knew how to do basic housekeeping jobs when they left home.

When is your daughter ready to wash and fold her own clothes? We have seen sweaters come out of the washing machine so small they looked like doll clothes, even though we cautioned, "Look at the label before you wash it. If the sweater has to be dry-cleaned, we'll take it to the cleaners." We've also noticed pink underwear that had been white before it was washed with a maroon sweatshirt. Mistakes are part of the process. Too often college students bring their dirty clothes home for Mom to wash. We certainly didn't want this to occur!

5. Money

Some teens have a built-in knack for managing money; others have a knack for spending it! We started by letting our teens manage their money for school supplies and lunches. Once they showed signs of maturing, we added shopping for clothes, and progressed from weekly allowances to monthly allowances.

We also included expectations about part-time and summer jobs in this area. At thirteen, one teen mowed yards during the summer. At fourteen, two of our teens worked as counselors at a Scout camp. It can be difficult for a teen to get a steady job until he or she is sixteen, but we felt they learned much through these working experiences.

Again, the standards we set varied for each teen. With all the extracurricular activities, one teen simply could not work and still complete schoolwork. Working, however, kept another busy and out of trouble. Obviously the teen's responsibilities at home will be less if she is working.

If your daughter begins to work regularly, consider letting her open a checking account. You may want to suggest that a certain percentage of the money she earns be saved for college or a special purchase. (You could include this standard as a part of the Birthday Box.)

6. Social Life

To offset disappointment at not being able to date at thirteen, we put a tentative plan in their Birthday Boxes for when they could progress to group activities at fourteen and fifteen, and finally a single date at sixteen. Seeing that these privileges were just around the corner kept them from complaining too much. With parties, we initially wanted to know where they were and what adults were supervising. It helped that our teens could not yet drive, so we were involved in the logistics. As they grew older, we loosened up on needing to know everything, but we still enforced the curfew. You'll have to make decisions around dating and parties that reflect what's best for your daughter.

7. Spiritual Life

While you can't legislate what your teenager will or will not believe, you can influence her. You can provide reading material—but forcing her to read it may prove counterproductive. In the early teen years we tried to help our boys find interesting devotional material on their level. Check out your local Christian bookstore for devotional books and books on Christian beliefs and values. We did include in the Birthday Box reading at least one faith-based book each year. We also subscribed to a relevant cutting-edge Christian magazine for teens. No doubt there will be apps, blogs, or websites your daughter will also relate to. Ask her youth leader for some suggestions.

Also we included attending a youth conference or a church youth group ski trip in our boys' boxes. The youth group at your church can be a positive influence. But what if your teenager hates the youth group? We know some families who changed churches during the teen years just to find a good youth group for their adolescents. One mom included the privilege of choosing a church in the box for her daughter's fifteenth birthday because the daughter was very unhappy at the family's church. That year the daughter became very active in church for the first time simply because of her excellent new youth group.

Again, developing a plan when the teen is young and still receptive to parental input ensures a gradual transition from a parent's to a teen's own values and convictions.

8. Driving, Meal Preparation, and So On

Driving is a big privilege for a teen and often requires a full-fledged agreement within the Birthday Box structure. One parent in a group we facilitated drew up the following contract together with her daughter.

Kelly's Driving Contract

Seat Belts

- I must wear a seat belt when I drive, and so must any other passengers.

Passengers

- No more than two people in the front seat (including me).
- No more than three people in the back.

Driving Range

- I can drive only within a twenty-mile radius, unless accompanied by an adult.

Maintaining Grades

- Grades must stay above a B average.

Consequences of Breaking Contract

- If grades are below a B average, the car is taken away for all social events until grades improve.
- Any speeding or parking tickets I get, I pay for myself.

Miscellaneous

- No texting or using a phone while driving!
- I will always let my parent know where I'm going to be.
- No one else shall drive the car.
- No one under the influence of alcohol may ride in the car. (We realize exceptions can happen when the only safe way for the teen to get home is to become the designated driver, but we would encourage parents to have the general guideline to not allow friends who are drinking to ride with them.)

One Mom's Experience

We had a driving contract for our daughter, Leah, but she was not excited about it. She told us she polled three people at school and they all thought it was "lame." I asked her who she polled, and she said that was confidential information. She was so mad about the contract that when she got it, she read through it like an attorney. Then she said, "I will sign it but I will not date it." She had to have the last word. We still have an undated contract, but it is still in place. And to this point, she has had no accidents.

You may also want to include other areas in your teen's Birthday Box, such as learning how to change a flat tire or getting certificated in CPR. You might want to include reading a book about investments and making a first small investment in the stock market. Whatever areas you choose to include, the goal is the same: to develop the teen's competence to function productively in the adult world.

At the end of this chapter you will find a guide to help you design your own plan of release.

Monitoring the Box

Plan a quarterly or six-month evaluation with your teen to discuss how she is doing. If your daughter lacks self-discipline, you may want to get together more often.

One of our sons kept asking, "How am I doing?" Since he was doing very well, we hadn't mentioned the box. After his comment, we realized he needed some positive feedback, so we began commenting occasionally, "You're doing a great job of keeping up with your homework."

What if your daughter doesn't carry through with the responsibilities or abuses the privileges? If she fails in one area, just repeat that area the next year. Remember, your teen wants new privileges. Once she understands they are accompanied by responsibilities, we hope she will not let you down.

One of our teenagers was the classic academic underachiever even though he was bright, so we made achieving a B average a requirement for getting his driver's license.

"Well, since I grew up in Austria, where you can't drive until you're eighteen, it's no big deal if I don't get my license," he replied.

But when his friends began to get their licenses, his attitude changed. Suddenly, his grades began to improve.

With one son we found we needed to be flexible. Once we saw improvement in his grades and his attitude toward his studies, we allowed him to get his license, even though he did not have a B average. But his driving was limited to work and to youth activities. A year later he finally achieved a B average, and we received the good student discount on our insurance.

A caution: Before you tie grades into privileges, ask yourself, "What is reasonable for my teen?" Some kids work harder to maintain a steady C average than others do to make straight As.

Our teens knew that their progress toward new freedoms depended upon four factors: overall attitude, spiritual growth, academics, and how well they managed the box.

Excelling in an area can speed up some privileges. For instance, if your daughter has been a good manager of finances from an early age, she might have her own debit card earlier than another sibling.

Alternative Approaches

You may want to begin the Birthday Box at eleven or twelve, or perhaps your teen will enjoy the box at thirteen but not again at fourteen, or will not cooperate if the Birthday Box is begun at fifteen. Some of the parents in our parenting groups and seminars adapted it as a High School Box with freshman, sophomore, junior, and senior privileges and responsibilities.

One mom learned about Project Thirteen and the Birthday Box right before her daughter's fourteenth birthday, so she combined the two to create Robin's Steps to Adulthood. The important thing is to set up a well-defined, progressive structure for increasing responsibilities and privileges each year.

Robin's Steps to Adulthood

1. You may choose your clothes and hairstyle.

2. Your homework will no longer be supervised, but we will be glad to help if asked.

3. Your bedtime is extended until 10:30 p.m. on school nights.

4. You will receive a $60 allowance a month for spending money and school obligations. Extra money may be earned by doing yard or housework.

5. Your room is now your responsibility. Mom has the right to refuse to allow friends to visit if your room isn't clean.

6. You are responsible for the care of your clothes. Mom will teach you how to wash, dry, and fold your clothing.

I know you can do it. I love you.
Mom

Robin hung the document on her bedroom wall and worked hard to achieve these responsibilities. But our friend's story doesn't end there. When Robin's older brother, sixteen-year-old Curt, celebrated his birthday, she took him out to dinner and discussed what he still needed to learn before he left home in approximately twenty-four months. Together they made a list, and now he is taking care of his clothes and, among other things, learning how to cook basic foods.

Her nine-year-old daughter watched this process and decided to get a head start. That summer she listed her own goals, one of which was to place in an event in the city swim meet. She not only placed in several events, but she also received the Most Improved Swimmer award for her local swim team.

"Megan was the only swimmer in our club that made and met her personal goals," her coach told her mother at the awards dinner.

Why Not Take a Chance?

Wise parents begin working toward their offspring's independence almost from the moment the child is born. Just as you hand the baby a spoon for eating, knowing he or she will probably plaster the wall with food, so you take risks all along the path. Releasing areas of responsibility can eliminate much frustration for both the teen and parent. Why not take the chance? Go on and give your adolescent a Birthday Box!

Establishing Teenage Birthday Boxes

1. Brainstorm your categories and list all the things your daughter needs to know in each area before she leaves home.

2. By each area, put when you think she will be ready to assume the responsibility.

3. Sketch or type two box diagrams. Insert the different areas and potential progression on each copy and give one to your daughter.

4. Be open to discussion. Let your daughter co-create her Birthday Box progression. Once you've agreed on your plan, remain open to annual tweaks that may need to take place.

5. Give her an actual Birthday Box container and present her with the first year's challenge cards and the diagram

of the overall plan. Each year on her birthday, present her with a new set of cards for that year. Review, refine, and celebrate her progress!

6. Keep the following questions in mind:

    A. Am I releasing too much or not enough freedom to my daughter?

    B. Am I giving her too much or not enough responsibility?

While statistics indicate that more and more kids are living at home in their twenties or thirties (or moving back home after college), our challenge to you is to use the upcoming teenage years to help prepare your daughter for adulthood come eighteen, so she can survive and thrive on her own at college and beyond. The two projects described in this chapter capture the essence of the concepts presented throughout the book while offering practical guidance for putting them into practice. Whether you take all or just some of these ideas, we wish you the very best as you journey with your daughter on her transition from tween to teen to young adult!

Notes

Conversation 1: The Big-Picture Talk

1. Richard Fry, "A Rising Share of Young Adults Live in Their Parents' Home," Pew Research Center, August 1, 2013, http://www.pewsocialtrends.org/2013/08/01/a-rising-share-of-young-adults-live-in-their-parents-home/.

2. James Dobson, "Some Battles with Adolescents Not Worth Waging War," *The Knoxville News-Sentinel*, October 31, 1998 B4.

Conversation 2: The Friends Talk

1. Lisa Damour, "The Emotional Whiplash of Parenting a Teenager," *The New York Times*, July 13, 2014, http://parenting.blogs.nytimes.com/2014/07/13/the-emotional-whiplash-of-parenting-a-teenager/.

2. Derek Thompson, "How Teenagers Spend Money," *The Atlantic*, April 12, 2013, http://www.theatlantic.com/business/archive/2013/04/how-teenagers-spend-money/274949/.

3. Mary Pipher, *Reviving Ophelia* (New York: Ballantine Books, 1995), 73, 83.

4. P. T. Costa Jr. and R. R. McCrae, *Revised NEO Personality Inventory (NEO-PI-R) and NEO Five-Factor Inventory (NEO-FFI) Manual* (Odessa, FL: Psychological Assessment Resources, 1992).

5. Merton and Irene Strommen, *Five Cries of Parents* (New York: Harper & Row, 1985), 6.

6. Josh Wiley, "Bible Verses About Friendship: 20 Good Scripture Quotes," What Christians Want to Know, May 1, 2011, http://www.whatchristianswanttoknow.com/bible-verses-about-friendship-20-good-scripture-quotes/.

Conversation 3: The Academics Talk

1. CareerBuilder, August 18, 2011, www.careerbuilder.com/share/aboutus/pr essreleasesdetail.aspx?id=pr652&sd=8/18/2011&ed=8/18/2099&siteid=cbpr&s c_cmp1=cb_pr652_.

2. K. E. Ablard and W. D. Parker, "Parents' Achievement Goals and Perfectionism in Their Academically Talented Children," *Journal of Youth and Adolescence* 26, no. 6 (December 1997): 651–667.

Conversation 4: The Body Talk

1. David Walsh, *Why Do They Act That Way? A Survival Guide to the Adolescent Brain for You and Your Teen* (New York: Atria Publishing, 2014).

2. Mary Pipher, *Reviving Ophelia* (New York: Ballantine Books, 1995), 23–24.

3. "Body Image and Nutrition," *Teen Health and the Media*, accessed April 1, 2015, http://depts.washington.edu/thmedia/view.cgi?section=bodyimage&p age=fastfacts.

4. Cynthia Heald, *Becoming A Woman of Strength* (Colorado Springs: NavPress, 2012).

Conversation 5: The Faith Talk

1. James W. Fowler, *Stages of Faith* (New York: HarperCollins, 1981).

2. Warren Benson, *The Complete Book of Youth Ministry* (Chicago: Moody Press, 1995), 53.

3. B. Griffen and K. Powell, "I Doubt It: Making Space for Hard Questions," *Stickyfaith.org*, March 10, 2014, http://stickyfaith.org/articles/i-doubt-it.

4. Jim Candy, Brad M. Griffin, and Kara Powell, *Can I Ask That? 8 Hard Questions about God and Faith* (Pasadena, CA: Fuller Youth Institute, 2014).

Conversation 6: The Boys Talk

1. Luke Gilkerson, "How Many Women Are Hooked on Porn? 10 Stats that May Shock You," Covenant Eyes, August 30, 2013, http://www.covenanteyes.co m/2013/08/30/women-addicted-to-porn-stats/.

2. Ana Maria Arumi, "Nearly 3 in 10 Young Teens, 'Sexually Active,'" NBC News, January 31, 2005, http://www.nbcnews.com/id/6839072/t/nearly-young-t eens-sexually-active/#.VSu_zPA08uc.

3. S. M. Stanley, G. K. Rhoades, and H. J. Markman, "Sliding vs. Deciding: Inertia and the Premarital Cohabitation Effect," *Family Relations* 55 (2006): 499–509.

4. Patti Neighmond, "Cheap Drinks and Risk-Taking Fuel College Drinking Culture" NPR, September 8, 2014, http://www.npr.org/blogs/health/2014/09/08 /345877489/cheap-drinks-and-risk-taking-fuel-college-drinking-culture.

5. M. Mohler-Kuo, G. W. Dowdall, M. P. Koss, and H. Wechsler, "Correlates of Rape While Intoxicated in a National Sample of College Women," *Journal of Studies on Alcohol and Drugs* 65, no. 1 (January 2004): 37–45.

6. Dennis and Barbara Rainey, *Passport2Purity* (Little Rock, AR: FamilyLife Publishing, 2012).

Conversation 7: The Money Talk

1. "Young Adults and Teens Lead Growth Among Smartphone Owners," Nielson, September 10, 2012, http://www.nielsen.com/us/en/insights/news/2012/young-adults-and-teens-lead-growth-among-smartphone-owners.html.
2. "American Family Financial Statistics," July 9, 2014, http://www.statisticbrain.com/american-family-financial-statistics/.

Bonus Activities: Project Thirteen and Birthday Boxes

1. David and Claudia Arp, *Suddenly They're 13* (Grand Rapids, MI: Zondervan Publishing, 1999).

Peter J. Larson, PhD, is a licensed clinical psychologist and currently serves as the Marriage and Family Initiative Lead at Gloo, Inc. He is the coauthor of the PREPARE/ENRICH Customized Version and the Couple Checkup Inventory and book. Heather Larson, MS, has her master's degree in psychology. She is the founder of Bridgewell Coaching and works as a Christian relationship coach. She and Peter regularly teach and speak together. They are the hosts of the *10 Great Dates Before You Say "I Do"* DVD curriculum. The Larsons have been married for twenty years and have three children.

Claudia Arp and David Arp, MSW, are founders of Marriage Alive International, a groundbreaking ministry dedicated to providing resources and training to empower churches to help build better marriages. The Arps are authors of numerous books and video curricula, including the *10 Great Dates* series and *The Connected Family* and *Suddenly They're 13—Or the Art of Hugging a Cactus*. The Arps have appeared on the NBC *Today Show*, CBS *This Morning*, PBS, and *Focus on the Family*. Their work has been featured in publications such as *USA Today*, the *Washington Post*, *New York Times*, *Wall Street Journal*, and *Time* magazine. When they are not writing or speaking, you'll probably find them hiking trails in Northern Virginia, where they live, or in the Austrian Alps, where they love to hike. For more information, visit www.10greatdates.org.

More From the Larsons and the Arps

Visit 10greatdates.org for more information.

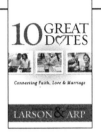

Amid your busy schedules, are you and your spouse finding time to connect? When was the last time you went on a date or had a good talk about faith? With this book, the Larsons and the Arps make it easy to do both with ten fun, creative date ideas, each centered on a spiritual theme. With the planning taken care of, you and your spouse can simply enjoy the time spent sharing what's important in life.

10 Great Dates: Connecting Faith, Love, and Marriage

Tired of the usual dinner-and-a-movie dates? Energize your marriage by getting out of your normal routine with the help of these 52 creative date ideas. From outdoor dates to out-on-the-town dates, you and your spouse will have no trouble finding the perfect date that fits your mood—all on a $10 budget! Each date includes easy preparation suggestions, tips for the date, talking points to enhance your conversations, and a Great Date takeaway.

$10 Dollar Dates: Connecting Love, Marriage, and Fun on a Budget